PROMETHEUS BOUND
By Æschylus
Translated by Thomas Medwin
&
Percy Bysshe Shelley

PROMETHEUS UNBOUND
By Percy Bysshe Shelley

Edited & with Foreword by John Lauritsen

PAGAN PRESS
2011

Prometheus Bound by Aeschylus, translated by Thomas Medwin & Percy Bysshe Shelley + **Prometheus Unbound** by Percy Bysshe Shelley. Edited and with Foreword by John Lauritsen.

Copyright • 2011 by Pagan Press.
http://paganpressbooks.com
Printed in the USA.
All rights reserved.

Correspondence can be sent to the editor:
  john_lauritsen@post.harvard.edu

Pagan Press was founded in 1982 to "publish books of interest to the intelligent gay man." *Pagan* here denotes the culture of Western Classical Antiquity.

Aeschylus.

Prometheus bound / by Aeschylus; translated by Thomas Medwin and Percy Bysshe Shelley. Prometheus unbound / by Percy Bysshe Shelley ; edited and with foreword by John Lauritsen – Dorchester, Massachusetts.: Pagan Press, 2011.

ISBN 978-0-943742-19-9

1. Prometheus (Greek deity) – Drama. I. Aeschylus, ca. 325/4-456/5 BC Prometheus bound. II. Shelley, Percy Bysshe, 1792-1822. Prometheus unbound. III. Medwin, Thomas, 1788-1869. IV. Lauritsen, John, 1939- .

882.01

Printed on acid-free paper. 2nd printing (revised) June 2012.
Library of Congress Control Number: 2011931256
ISBN 978-0-943742-19-9   paperback

CONTENTS

Thomas Jefferson Hogg on Shelley	4
Foreword	5
Bibliography/References	19
Argument for Prometheus Bound	22
Prometheus Bound by Aeschylus	24
Shelley's Preface to Prometheus Unbound	80
Prometheus Unbound by Shelley	87

APPENDIX
John Addington Symonds on Prometheus Unbound	202
Prometheus by Goethe	208
Notes on typefaces, editor, artist.	211

I knew Shelley more intimately than any man, but I never could discern in him any more than two fixed principles. The first was a strong, irrepressible love of liberty.... The second was an equally ardent love of toleration of all opinions, but more especially of religious opinions; of toleration, complete, entire, universal, unlimited; and, as a deduction and corollary from which latter principle, he felt an intense abhorrence of persecution of every kind, public or private.

– Thomas Jefferson Hogg
Life of Shelley, 1858.

Foreword [1]

When translations of the plays of Aeschylus were published in the 1830s, under the name of Thomas Medwin, they were critically acclaimed as "by far the best" into English, having "fire, spirit, and general correctness." One reviewer praised the translator for having:

> ... an admirable acquaintance with the language, style and sentiments of his author, a noble mastery over his own tongue, a thrilling sense of the beautiful and sublime, together with a thorough sympathy with the freshness and glory of the classical drama. (*The Literary Gazette*, 28 April 1832)

But these translations are virtually unknown now, either to classical scholars or teachers of English literature.

In this Foreword I shall argue that one of the greatest English poets, Percy Bysshe Shelley, was a full collaborator on the Aeschylus translations with his cousin, Thomas Medwin – that Shelley himself was the primary craftsman in composition – that these forgotten translations are in many ways superior to any done since.

Thomas Medwin (1788-1869), the son of a prosperous lawyer and landowner, was a cousin and life-long friend of Percy Bysshe Shelley, whose childhood home in West Sussex was only two miles away. After attending Syon House Academy in Isleworth and then a preparatory school, Medwin entered Oxford in 1805, and left several years later without a

---

[1] This book is a companion publication with Aeschylus: *Oresteia, the Medwin-Shelley translation* (Pagan Press 2011), and the present Foreword will necessarily repeat some of the information from that book.

degree. In 1812 he joined the 24th Light Dragoons, in which he did service in India until 1818, when the regiment was disbanded; he retired as a lieutenant on half pay.

In late 1819, when Medwin was living in Geneva, he discovered Shelley's early poetry, and became one of the first to grasp his genius. A letter from Shelley in 1820 urged Medwin to join him in Italy, "the Paradise of exiles, the retreat of Pariahs", and Medwin did so. Reunited after an absence of seven years, the two cousins collaborated intensely for four months in translating Greek and German.

Unfortunately, Shelley's second wife, Mary, became hostile to Medwin, perhaps because the two men would leave her alone as they went off to study together, or would discuss things in her presence that were beyond her ken, so she eventually drove Medwin away, stating in a letter to her stepsister, Claire Clairmont, that she and Shelley found him a "seccatura" (should have been *seccatore*: bore, nuisance) and "Common Place personified". In truth, Shelley never found Medwin boring or "common place", nor ever said an unkind word about him. Shelley later apologized to Medwin, and urged him to return to Pisa, which he did later in 1821. Medwin then met and became the friend and confidant of Byron, who had moved to Pisa to be with Shelley.

Medwin has been described by his biographer (Lovell) as "one of the most outrageously misrepresented men in all literary history." He has been denigrated by biographers for two main reasons: his Byron biography stepped on a lot of toes, and he was disliked by Mary Shelley, whose thoughtless remarks (including an absurd accusation of attempted blackmail) were believed and embellished upon by her over-zealous biographers. Medwin's life was indeed a mess: he was disinherited by his father, and lived the last half of his life in near poverty. Nevertheless, he was a good and prolific writer and a fine classical scholar. He was the first biographer of both Byron and Shelley, some of whose works would not have survived except for him. His considerable literary output included poems, short fiction, traveller's tales, a novel, and translations from Italian, German and Greek.

Percy Bysshe Shelley (1792-1822) is the subject of numerous biographies, few of which can be recommended without reservations. He was amazingly versatile – not only a major poet, but also a major novelist, essayist, playwright, and translator. "Shelley was a translator of extraordinary range and versatility, whose acquaintance with European literature makes most English poets between Dryden and Eliot look provincial." (Webb)

If Shelley has not been credited as a translator of Aeschylus, it is for want of surviving manuscripts – but we know that for years he worked on translating his plays. Shelley enjoyed translating orally, and in 1816 did all of *Prometheus Bound* for Byron. A journal note by Mary Shelley, his scribe, indicates that as early as 1817 Shelley was preparing a written translation of *Prometheus* ("Shelley translates Prometheus Desmotes and I write it."). In 1821 Shelley introduced Medwin to the plays of Aeschylus:

> During this winter, he translated to me the *Prometheus* of Æschylus, reading it as fluently as if written in French or Italian; and if there be any merit in my own version of that wonderful drama, which appeared together with the remaining Plays in Fraser, it is much due to the recollection of his words, which often flowed on line after

line in blank verse, into which very harmonious prose resolves itself naturally. (Medwin 1847, pp. 242-243)

This account cannot be entirely true. No doubt Shelley did read his translation of *Prometheus* to Medwin, but he would have done so from a written version – a manuscript, which Mary had already transcribed, from his dictation or handwriting. It is beyond belief that Shelley would have worked out a complete translation of *Prometheus* without committing it to writing – and after all, Mary's clerical services were readily available. It is absurd to imagine that the manifest Shelleyan presence in *Prometheus* and *Oresteia* is nothing more than Medwin's "recollection of his words" over a decade later. What happened to the manuscripts of Shelley's Aeschylus translations? The only plausible answer is that Medwin retained them – and it's probably best that he did. We cannot be sure that all of Shelley's works have survived. His masterful translation of Plato's dialogue, *The Banquet* (or *Symposium*), was not published complete and unexpurgated until 131 years after completion, and then "for private circulation" only. (Plato)

So then, the manuscripts of Shelley's Aeschylus translations were not lost or destroyed, but retained by Medwin, who used them for the translations he published in *Fraser's*, over a decade after Shelley's death. We can only speculate why Medwin failed to credit Shelley as a collaborator in the translations, rather than just as a mentor. Possibly he feared obstacles from Mary Shelley, who had taken charge of publishing her husband's works, although she was not his official literary executor. Or he may simply have wanted to boost his own literary career.

At any rate, the case that Shelley was a collaborator in the translations – that he was the primary craftsman in composing both dialogue passages, to be spoken, and verse passages, to be sung or chanted – is confirmed by the translations themselves.

Shelley's hand in the Aeschylus translations is apparent in the great variety of verse forms employed – and he was the master of more verse forms than any other poet in English. The translations contain unique and intricate verse forms, as well as traditional odes, sonnets, Spenserian stanzas, iambic pentameter, and even an unorthodox sestina – all crafted by a master poet. Medwin did write poetry, some of which is not bad, but he never demonstrated the versification technique that is brilliantly evident in the translations.

Shelley did not strive for a literal, word-for-word and line-by-line translation. He believed that a translator should fully understand the meaning of the original, and then re-create that meaning in English. Shelley did not attempt to replicate the exact verse form of the original, but to use whatever forms he found appropriate:

> A Moschus epigram is transformed into a sonnet, [Ode to] Mercury exchanges hexameter for ottava rima, and the other Homeric Hymns are rendered in couplets (just as Virgil appears in terza rima and Calderon and Goethe in blank verse). (Webb)

In his *Life of Percy Bysshe Shelley*, written a quarter-century after Shelley's death and a decade after the *Fraser's* publication of *Prometheus*, Medwin explains Shelley's philosophy of translation and his deliberate choice of English meters different from the Greek or German originals:

> Shelley's translations are of the highest order – so high, that all must regret they were so few. He alone of all men that the present age has produced, was fitted to take up Goethe's Mantle. But the best proof of the excellency of Shelley's version, is, that Goethe himself is said to have expressed his entire approbation of these scenes of Shelley's.
>
> The rock on which all have split who have attempted to render *Faust*, has been an overscrupulous regard to metrical arrangement, which he, with his exquisite taste, avoided. Others do not seem to have been aware that the genius of German and English poetry is so widely different, that what produces a magical effect in the metre of one language, appears namby-pamby and puerile in the other. Milton made the experiment in Horace's *Ode to Pyrrha*, – failed, and never made a second attempt. Bulwer tried to render Schiller line by line, which has given not only a stiffness to his version, but renders much of it obscure, not to say unintelligible. In his "*Ideale und das Leben*", I was at a loss to find the original. But I have been led too far out of my way. Shelley needs no justification. *Faust* yet remains to be translated; but who would venture to put anything he could produce in competition with Shelley's Hartz Mountain scene. "There is no greater mistake than to suppose" – I use Shelley's own words – "that the knowledge of a language is all that is required in a translator. He must be a poet, and as great a one as his original, in order to do justice to him." (Medwin 1847)

Aside from versification, Shelley's hand appears in favorite words and phrases of his. Suffice two examples: the unusual word "tottering" is used no fewer than four times in the Medwin-Shelley translation of *Prometheus*, as well as twice in *Oresteia*. "Totter", "tottered", or "tottering" are used in Shelley's other works – *The Cyclops, Rosalind and Helen, Ode to Liberty, The Cenci* (three times), *Laon and Cythna* (twice), and in the fragment, *The Waning Moon*.

Shelley was keen on the words *glut* and *maw*, inspired by a couplet in Milton:

So death Shall be deceav'd his glut, and with us two
Be forc'd to satisfie his Rav'nous Maw. (PL, X, ll. 990-91)

The words are used to stunning effect in the Medwin-Shelley translation of *Prometheus Bound*:

The blood-delighting vulture, shall be sent
To tear your body piecemeal, and to glut
His ravenous maw by preying on your vitals

Shelley's own poem, *Prometheus Unbound*, has this couplet:

These are Jove's tempest-walking hounds,
Whom he gluts with groans and blood[2]

Maw is used repeatedly in Shelley's poetry: four times in his translation of the Euripides satyr play, *Cyclops*, twice in

---

[2]Panthea speaking, *Prometheus Unbound*, Act I, lines 330-31.

Oedipus, and once in *Verses on a Cat*. *Glut/gluts/glutted* is used in *The Cenci, To Death, Peter Bell the Third, Queen Mab, A Vision of the Sea, Alastor, Falsehood and Vice: A Dialogue, Laon and Cythna*, and in his juvenile novel, *St. Irvyne*.

Shelley used a glut-maw phrase in his juvenile poem, *Revenge*: "Alone will I glut its all conquering maw."[3] – and memorably in *Frankenstein*: "I will glut the maw of death."[4]

Vitality is the great virtue of the Medwin-Shelley translations of Aeschylus. A true translation is not a decoding operation – not a mere transfer of information from one language to another – but **re-creating** the energy, wit, irony, and pathos of the original. The Shelleyan philosophy of translation is shared by Burton Raffel, in a note accompanying his superb translation of *Beowulf*.

> ... no poem in translation is the original from which it takes its life; there must be distortion, to a greater or lesser degree, simply by definition. The greatest sin a translator can commit, accordingly, is to fail to breathe life into his re-creation. He can never breathe life into it if he is unable to force himself away from the original, and far enough away so that he can be close in spirit and yet be free to create in the new linguistic medium. (Raffel 1971)

Shelley's hand is as unmistakable in the pentameter dialogue as in the rhymed verse passages, for he was a master

---

[3] "Revenge" in *Original Poetry by Victor and Cazire*, line 20.

[4] The Monster is threatening his creator (*Frankenstein*, Vol. II, ch. 2). See Lauritsen 2007 for the case that Percy Bysshe Shelley is the true author of *Frankenstein*.

of dialogue. Shelley's felicity of dialogue is shown in his verse plays, *The Cenci* and *Prometheus Unbound*; in his novels, *Zastrozzi*, *St. Irvyne*, and *Frankenstein*; in his translation of Plato's dialogue, *The Banquet*; and in *Julian and Maddalo* and other poems.

The dialogue passages of the Medwin-Shelley translation show the power and versatility, the congenial formality, of English pentameter to convey speech. Good readers will instinctively read the lines aloud, or at least *hear* them inside their heads. This is a translation for actors – actors who can do justice to the language of Shakespeare.

Although I have argued that Shelley was the primary craftsman in composing this translation, I would not claim it as his work alone. In a true collaboration – and I have done them – there will not be a single passage, or sentence or word, that an outsider could say with certainty were written by one particular collaborator. Granted, there could be a division of labor: in translation, one collaborator might concentrate on the Greek and the other on composing the English – or in a non-fiction work, each collaborator might write certain sections. But even so, the collaborators would go over each other's work, so that words of both collaborators might appear within a single line or sentence.

Shelley's life was motivated by a love of liberty and a hatred of persecution, as attested by his friend, Thomas Jefferson Hogg (page 4). Hence, his commitment to the theme of Prometheus: the Freethinker intransigently rebelling against Tyranny. Neither in the Medwin-Shelley translation of *Prometheus Bound*, nor in Shelley's own *Prometheus Unbound*, does the hero regret his actions in bringing fire and enlightenment to mankind.

Shelley's Prometheus Unbound

Prometheus Bound of Aeschylus is only the second play of what was once a trilogy. Only a few fragments of the first and third plays survive – just enough to suggest that in the end Prometheus was freed after a reconciliation with Zeus/Jove. To Shelley this was unacceptable. In his *Preface* to his own poem, *Prometheus Unbound*, he states: "I was averse from a catastrophe so feeble as that of reconciling the Champion with the Oppressor of mankind." Accordingly, the forces of tyranny are overthrown, and a free and beautiful era is ushered in – an era of "Gentleness, Virtue, Wisdom, and Endurance". Nevertheless, in his *Preface* Shelley emphatically denies that his poem is intended solely to inculcate political ideas:

> "But it is a mistake to suppose that I dedicate my poetical compositions solely to the direct enforcement of reform, or that I consider them in any degree as containing a reasoned system on the theory of human life. Didactic poetry is my abhorrence; nothing can be equally well expressed in prose that is not tedious and supererogatory in verse."

Shelley's *Prometheus Unbound* is considered his masterpiece, and was his favorite of his own poems. It was composed in Italy between 1818 and 1819, and first published in London in 1820. Reception was mixed from the very beginning. While some critics found the poem obscure, or were hostile to Shelley's perceived political views, most appreciated its poetic beauty.

In his Introduction to the Variorum Edition, Lawrence John Zillman devotes a full 76 pages to summarizing critical opinion, from 1820 to the mid-20th century:

> "With the publication of the poem there began the growth of that forest of criticism which it is frequently difficult to see because of the trees of prejudice, special pleading, and sheer obtuseness with which it is planted." (Zillman, p. 36)

Difficult as *Prometheus Unbound* may be, champions of the poem denied it was obscure or unintelligible. R.A. Holland suggested, "what appears its author's mysticism may be the student's mistiness of apprehension.... Poetry has other offices than amusement." [5]

William Rossetti bluntly stated:

> "Though you cannot read *Prometheus Unbound*, I can. I have read it, and do read it, and this with ever-increasing admiration, wonder, and insight into its depth of beauty. Therefore it is a poem written, if not for you and yours, still for me and mine, and I am quite justified in regarding it as a masterpiece." [6]

Although many artists have depicted Prometheus as a mature man, often bearded, both Aeschylus and Shelley saw him as a beautiful youth. Despite belonging to an older generation of deities, Prometheus is eternally young and

---

[5] "Soul of Shelley", 1876; quoted in Zillman, p. 42.

[6] "Prometheus as Poem", 1887; quoted in Zillman, p. 42.

beautiful – as portrayed by Jean-Louis-Cesar Lair in the painting on the cover of this book. Some descriptions of Prometheus in Shelley's *Prometheus Unbound* are erotic (*e.g.*, Panthea's description of Prometheus in Act II, lines 62 *et seq.*).

The versecraft of *Prometheus Unbound* warrants comment, especially in comparison with that of the Aeschylus translations. Vida Scudder identified no fewer than 36 distinct verse forms:

> Blank verse rises into the long, passionate swing of the anapaest, or is broken by the flute-like notes of short trochaic lines, or relieved by the half-lyrical effect of rhymed endings.... the variety of metres is marvelous. Thirty-six distinct verse-forms are to be found, besides the blank verse. These forms are usually simple; but at times the versification-scheme is as complex as that of the most elaborate odes of Dryden or Collins. [7]

Comparing the versification in *Prometheus Unbound* with that in the Aeschylus translations can lead to only one conclusion: all were composed by the same poet.

Shelley's blank verse, as used in dialogue passages, also drew praise. Stopford Brooke said that Shelley:

> "used blank verse as if it were his natural tongue. It is easy, weighty, flowing, well paused, close knit, or let free, exactly as the mind within him drove, or the subject claimed." [8]

---

[7] Vida Scudder, *Prometheus Unbound*, Boston 1892; quoted in Zillman, p. 55.

[8] "Inaugural Address", 1886; quoted in Zillman, p. 55.

Appendix

John Addington Symonds, in an excerpt from his book on Shelley, discusses the ideas and poetic qualities of *Prometheus Unbound*. A 1789 poem by Johann Wolfgang von Goethe, *Prometheus*, translated from German by myself, is almost a precursor of Shelley's, expressing a similar hatred for tyranny and contempt for religion.

Text of the translation

The first translation of *Prometheus Bound* under Medwin's byline, which I have not seen, was in Siena (1827). It was then published as a book (London 1832) and in *Fraser's Magazine* (1837). In general, the *Fraser's* version is superior, and has been used here – though it is not without errors, which have been silently corrected. Footnotes indicate differences between the two versions.

In their translations of *Prometheus Bound* and of the three *Oresteia* plays, Medwin and Shelley used Roman names for the Greek Gods: Mercury for Hermes, Jove for Zeus, Minerva for Athena, and so on. Classical scholars frown on this practice, and for good reason: the Greek and Roman religious systems were different, and the Aeschylus plays are Greek, not Roman.

In my editing of the *Oresteia* translation, I changed the Roman names back to Greek in the dialogue passages, while retaining them – if necessary for rhyme or meter – in the verse passages. This was desirable for a number of reasons, not least of which was the cognate relationship between Athena and Athens, and between Ares and Areopagus/Areopagites – relationships which are lost if the Roman names are used: Minerva for Athena or Mars for Ares.

However, in the present work, I have left the Roman names unchanged, feeling that they are firmly embedded in the translation verse, and also because the Roman names are used in Shelley's own work, *Prometheus Unbound*.

The text of *Prometheus Unbound* follows Hutchinson.

I conclude this *Foreword* with the hope that the Medwin-Shelley translations will receive the performances they deserve, that English Literature and Classics departments will appreciate their excellence, and that the reader of this book will enjoy them as much as I have.

John Lauritsen
Boston 2011

Bibliography/References

Edmund Blunden, *Shelley: A Life Story*, 1946.
  The best short biography of Shelley. Blunden brings a poet's understanding to Shelley's life and poetry.

Richard Holmes, *Shelley: The Pursuit*, 1974.
  Still the best full-length biography of Shelley.

John Lauritsen, *The Man Who Wrote Frankenstein*, 2007.
  Frankenstein is a great work of literature, and Percy Bysshe Shelley is the true author.

Ernest J. Lovell, Jr, *Captain Medwin: Friend of Byron and Shelley*, 1962.
  Lovell ably defends "one of the most outrageously misrepresented men in all literary history."

Thomas Medwin, *The Life of Percy Bysshe Shelley*, 1847; New, expanded edition edited by H. Buxton Forman, 1913.
  Although Medwin made some minor mistakes, he brought Shelley to life. Some of Shelley's works would never have survived, had it not been for Medwin.

  – *Conversations of Lord Byron – Revised with a New Preface by the Author* (E.J. Lovell, Jr., Ed.) Princeton UP. 1966. Originally published in 1824.

James A. Notopoulos, *The Platonism of Shelley*, 1949.
  Notable especially for Notopoulos's analysis of Shelley's translation of Plato's dialogue, *The Banquet* (or *Symposium*).

Michael O'Neill, "Percy Bysshe Shelley, *Prometheus Unbound*". In Duncan Wu, editor: *A Companion to Romanticism*, 1998.

Laurence Perrine, *Sound and Sense: An Introduction to Poetry*, 1956.
   Especially pertinent: how to read poetry, and how to distinguish the bad from the good.

Plato, *The Banquet* (Symposium), translated by Percy Bysshe Shelley, with Foreword by John Lauritsen, 2001.
   Shelley's masterpiece of translation was first suppressed and then bowdlerized – not published in its entirety until 1931, and then in an edition of 100 copies intended "for private circulation only" (Ingpen). The Pagan Press edition of 2001 represents the first and only public edition of the translation, complete and unexpurgated, with Shelley's accompanying essay, "A Discourse on the Manners of the Antient Greeks".

Burton Raffel, translator, *Beowulf*, 1971.

Percy Bysshe Shelley, *The Complete Poetry of Percy Bysshe Shelley*, edited by Donald H. Reiman and Neil Fraistat, Volume One, 2000. Volume Two, 2004.

   – *The Letters of Percy Bysshe Shelley*, edited by Frederick L. Jones, 2 vols., 1964.

   – *Poetical Works*, edited by Thomas Hutchinson; a new edition, corrected by G.M. Matthews, 1970.

— *Shelley's Prose, or The Trumpet of a Prophecy*, edited by David Lee Clark, 1988.

— *Zastrozzi, A Romance & St. Irvyne; or, The Rosicrucian: a Romance*, edited by Stephen C. Behrendt, 2002.

Robert Metcalf Smith, *The Shelley Legend*, 1945.
   Rather rough, but essential for its thesis, that Mary Shelley and her daughter-in-law, Jane, Lady Shelley, fabricated a myth: "the fraudulent and mistaken efforts to turn the romantic, pagan Shelley, as Hogg, Peacock, and Trelawny knew him in the flesh, into a Victorian angel suitable for enshrinement among the gods of respectability and convention."

John Addington Symonds, *Shelley*, 1887.

Lewis Turco, *The Book of Forms*, 1968.
   This concisely explains over 175 specific verse forms that are traditional in Anglo-American prosody. It also covers metrics, sonics and the figurative language of poetry.

Timothy Webb, *The violet in the crucible: Shelley and translation*, 1976.
   Shelley as translator – only equalled, if at all, by Pope and Dryden.

Lawrence John Zillman, *Shelley's Prometheus Unbound: A Variorum Edition*, 1959.

ARGUMENT [1]

THE chained Prometheus is the representation of constancy under suffering, and that the never-ending suffering of a God. Though he is exiled to a naked rock on the shore of the encircling ocean, this drama still embraces the world, the Olympus of the Gods, and the earth of mortals; all scarcely yet reposing in a secure state above the dread abyss of the dark Titanian powers. This idea of a self-devoting divinity has been mysteriously inculcated in many religions, as a confused foreboding of the true; here, however, it appears in a most alarming contrast with the consolations of revelation. For Prometheus does not suffer in an understanding with the powers by whom the world is governed, but he atones for his disobedience, and that disobedience consists in nothing but the attempt to give perfection to the human race. He is thus an image of human nature itself, endowed with a miserable foresight, and bound down to a narrow existence, without an ally, and with nothing to oppose to the combined and inexorable powers of nature, but an unshaken will, and the consciousness of elevated claims.

The poet has contrived in a masterly manner to introduce variety and progress into that which in itself was determinately fixed, and gives us a scale, for the measurement of the matchless power of his Titans, in the objects by which he has surrounded them. We have first the silence of Prometheus while he is chained down under the harsh

---

[1] This **Argument** accompanied the translation in the London 1832 book, but was omitted in the 1837 publication in *Fraser's Magazine*. Medwin's note: I make no apology for taking this argument from Black's translation of Schlegel's admirable treatise on dramatic literature.

inspection of Strength and Force, whose threats serve only to excite a useless compassion in Vulcan, who carries them into execution; then his solitary complaints, the arrival of the tender Ocean-nymphs, whose kind and disheartening sympathy induces him to give vent to his feelings, to relate the causes of his fate, and to reveal the future, though with prudent reserve he reveals it only in part; the visit of the ancient Oceanus, a kindred God of the race of the Titans, who, under the pretext of a zealous attachment to his cause, advises him to submission towards Jupiter, and who on that account is dismissed with contempt; the introduction of the raving Io, the victim of the same tyranny from which Prometheus suffers, his prophecy of the wanderings to which she is still doomed, and the fate which at last awaits her, connected in some degree with his own, as from her blood he is to derive a deliverer after the lapse of many ages; the appearance of Mercury as the messenger of the tyrant of the world, who with threats commands him to disclose the secret by which Jupiter may remain on his throne secure from the malice of fate, and lastly the yawning of the ground before Prometheus has well declared his refusal, amidst thunder and lightning, storm, and earthquake, by which he himself, and the rock to which he is chained, are swallowed up in the abyss of the nether world.

PROMETHEUS BOUND: FROM ÆSCHYLUS

Translated by Thomas Medwin & Percy Bysshe Shelley

Dramatis Personæ

Prometheus.
Strength.
Force.
Vulcan.
Oceanus.
Mercury.
Io.

Chorus of Ocean Nymphs.

STRENGTH. FORCE. VULCAN. PROMETHEUS.

    Strength. Behold us at the furthest verge of earth !
A Scythian waste of solitudes, untrod,
And uninhabitable by mortals. Vulcan !
Commissioned by the Father, to these rocks,
Of summits inaccessible, with chains
Indissolubly interlinked, 'tis thine
To bind this evil-doer ! – his transgression [1]
Fell most on thee, in that he stole, and gave
Thy share – fire's all-inventive ray – to man: [2]

---

[1] In the London 1832 book this line is: *This evil-doer, Vulcan ! – his transgression*. This line gives the wrong impression that the evil-doer is Vulcan, rather than Prometheus; it was corrected in the present text, which is that of *Fraser's Magazine*, 1837.

[2] The 1832 book has *mortals* instead of *man*.

Fit punishment, and worthy of the gods, [3]
Must expiate such offence; that he may learn
The all-mightiness of Jove, respect his rule,
And cease from over-benefiting clay. [4]

    Vul. Strength ! and thou, Force ! by you Jove's ordinance
Has been thus far completed – in your path
As yet I've thrown no obstacle. But though
I have the hand, I lack the heart, to bind
To this crag, tempest-buffeted, a god, [5]
A fellow-deity; still, not the less,
Dire irresistible necessity
Constrains me to the task; for hard it were
To strive against the Omnipotent ... Yet hear !
Thou son of Themis ! full of truth, thyself,
And stern resolve ! forgive me, that with these
Irrefragable chains, against my will,
And against thine, I am compelled to bind thee
To this inclement promontory's side;
Where never sound of human voice, nor form
Nor face of man shalt thou perceive, but where
Unsheltered from the burning sun, its flame
Shall change thy bloom of beauty; and to thee

---

[3] The 1832 book has *god* and *gods* in upper case.

[4] 1832 book: *man* instead of *clay*.

[5] 1832 book:
  Stern powers! by you the ordinance of Jove
  Has been thus far completed – and as yet
  There have been found no obstacles; but I
  Feel not the force, had I the heart, to bind
  To this crag, tempest-buffeted, a God.

26   Æschylus

The starry veil of night shall only bring
A longing after day, and day will come
To make thee wish it done, when it shall melt.
The hoar-frost of the morn from thy numbed limbs,
Making thee ever deem the present worst,
In that thine agony; nor is there born
Who can or would relieve thee. This the fruit
Of thy philanthropy – and thou, a god,
To brave the anger of the gods – for whom?
For man ! to break for him all laws divine,
And lavish on mortality the gifts,
The immortal gifts, of gods: and what hast thou
Received for all thy benefits? This rock – [6]
This joyless, herbless rock, where to keep watch,
Where never to close eye, or to bend knee,
Shalt thou be fixed erect, and for all sounds
Of harmony divine, send forth a voice
Of wailing and despair, that ill become [7]
A son of Heaven. Hast thou found out at last
The inexorable mind of Jove, and learnt
All new in power are harsh?
    Strength.   Well, well ! and if
It be so, as you say, what's that to you?
Why waste your time in empty talk and pity?
Thou, of all gods, oughtest to hate the most

---

[6] In 1832 book:
  And lavish the immortal gifts of Gods
  On recreant mortality; and now,
  What hast thou in exchange for all delights -

[7] In 1832 book: Of never-ending wail, that ill becomes

This execrable god, who stole thy gift,
And gave't to man.
    Vul.   Your language well becomes you;
You never felt the ties of blood, nor knew
The charms of social intercourse.
    Strength.   That I grant;
Nathless, consider who the Father is,
And what he is, before you thwart his will.
Doth not the fear of Jove outweigh the love
Of blood and fellowship? [8]
    Vul.   Still I pity him !
But you were made for any tyrant's acts;
Your heart is shut to all the soft affections.
    Strength. Were my heart other than it is, 'twere vain
To whine for him; and, trust me, it were best [9]
That you should not waste fruitlessly the time: [10]
Of what avail are words?
    Vul.   Alas ! that I
Should live to curse the works of my own hands,
To hate my art itself.
    Strength.   And why hate it?
Your art, forsooth ! Pray, tell me how your art's
To blame in this?
    Vul.   Would that my attribute
Had fallen on other than myself !
    Strength.   Admit

---

[8] 1832: Of all your kindred?

[9] In 1832 book: ... it is best

[10] 1832: You should not waste your time thus fruitlessly:

You could exchange, what would that profit you?
Would you be free? To be lord of himself
Is Jove's, and only Jove's, prerogative. [11]
    Vul. I know it well, nor can gainsay your words.
    Strength. Wind, then, these chains about him that the
        Father [12]
May find no cause to tax you with delay.
    Vul. See here the ready manacles!
    Strength.   Then take,
And with your pincers strain them round his wrists:
Use all your might; then nail him to the rock.
    Vul. I have advanced the work – and not in vain.
    Strength. Strike hard, clinch closer, nor relax your gripe; [13]
His excellent skill in mischief could untwist
Links seemingly inextricable.
    Vul.   That
Which knits this arm no power of his shall loosen.
    Strength. Clench this as fast, to prove that all his art
And wisdom yields to that of Jove.
    Vul.   Save him,
None else shall justly blame my handiwork.
    Strength. The jagged jaws of the adamantine belt
Lock round his chest, and firmly close the teeth.
    Vul. Oimé! Oimé! Prometheus! how I groan,
In thinking of the agonies you must bear.
    Strength. What, dally still, and throw away your groans

---

[11] 1832: no commas.

[12] 1832: Wind then these chains about him, that your father

[13] 1832: Strike hard, clinch closer, unrelax your gripe,

Upon Jove's enemies: save them, for you soon
May want them for yourself.
 Vul.   Behold
A spectacle of horror every eye
Must dread to look upon !
 Strength.   I see but him
Meeting with his deserts: but come – proceed !
Why are the gyves not fitted to his hips?
 Vul. Alas, it must be so ! But 'tis not thine
Too harshly to enforce the cruel order. [14]
 Strength. Not mine ! – too harshly ! – but I tell thee,
Vulcan,
I'll raise my voice to yet a higher pitch,
If ... lower ..... still lower ..... now compress the rings,
And gird them round his legs.
 Vul.   That too is done;
The task itself is light.
 Strength.   Rivet the fetters:
The exacter of this work's a hard task-master,
Difficult to please.
 Vul.   Your features and your words
Suit well together.
 Strength.   Keep your womanish nature:
For me, I would not change my fearless heart,
All proud and hard as you may wrongly deem it,
For one so weak of purpose.

---

[14] 1832 has three lines here:
 It must be so .... for dire necessity,
 Alas ! constrains me, but it is not thine
 Too harshly to enforce the cruel order.

    Vul.   Let us go; [15]
He's chained and bound in sinew, joint, and limb.
    Strength. Here vent your curses, and the gifts of gods
Steal, if thou canst, and lavish them on man.
Can mortals profit thee in aught, or soothe
A portion of the pangs incurred for them?
Falsely the gods have called thee provident:
Need were of other providence than thine own
To loose the chains that have been wound about thee.
    Pro. (*solus*). Best and divinest air! ye swift-winged winds!
Ye river-springs! and ocean-billows! ye
That countless in your multitudes laugh out
With long loud peals – exulting to be free!
Earth, universal mother of all life!
And thou, O sun, whose eye pierces all nature,
You I invoke! look how and what I suffer,[16]
From gods, a god! I call on you! Behold
What infinite agonies I have to bear,
Infinite ages! Witness what vile chains
This new-raised king of the gods has forged for me!
Ai! Ai! the present, and the coming lot!
Eternity of agonies! wo for ever![17]
And must it last for ever – know no respite?
What do I say? and was the future hid
From my foreknowledge? did I not foresee
All that should come upon me? Let me, then,

---

[15] 1832: Let us not go,

[16] 1832: You I invoke! look on me, what I suffer,

[17] 1832: woe for wo.

Bear, as becomes me best, the doom of fate,
Bowing to the inexorable might
Of stern necessity. Wretch that I am!
Where shall I look for fortitude to bear
In silence, or what solace can I seek
In telling all I bear. Why am I yoked
With these inevitable ills? Alas,
Was not my gift a blessing to mankind?
True! I for them from heaven's own fountain stole
A spark of fire. But did not fire give light,
Teaching all arts to render less the sum
Of human misery, and enable man
The better to support the load of being?
This is the front of my offence ... and now,
What is the sentence I am doomed to meet?
Indissoluble chains, and to converse
With everlasting groans, prisoned beneath
This dungeon-vault of the air!
Wo, wo, for ever!

[The CHORUS *are seen in the distance.*]

Hist! hark! What do I hear? Again!
What echoes steal along – what means that sound?
Whence are those odours, filling every sense?
Come they from earth, or heaven?
What art thou? – God or man, [18]

---

[18] 1832:
  Whence are those odors sweeter than all sound
  Of voice or instrument, filling every sense –
  Come they from earth or heaven?

Or creature of the elements composed
Of some mixed essence? Let me question why
Thou thus dost visit earth's extremest bound?
What wouldst thou here? With me ... say, art thou come
To look upon my woes – perhaps to insult?
Behold, whoe'er thou art, a sight of horror
That eye ne'er saw ! Look, if thou darest, on me,
Hateful to Jove, and whom the inhabitants
Of heaven hate, not the less – on me, a being [19]
Of an immortal nature, exiled from
The abodes of immortality, and bound
For having loved mankind with too much love –
Bound, as you see – this was my only crime.
Wo's me ! again what onward-rustling plumes [20]
Winnow the yielding air with the quick stroke
Of alternating pinions? Near ! more near !
All that approaches now, I fear ! I fear !

The CHORUS *enter.*

    Cho. Fear not ! fear not ! we come ! we come !
Sailing in our air-borne ship,
To this eagle height, from our ocean home,
On a voyage of sweet companionship;

    And what art thou, or God, or man,

[19] 1832:
    Hated by Jove, and no less hateful to
    The inhabitants of Heaven, on me, a Being

[20] 1832: woe's me. Consistently spelled *woe* in 1832 and *wo* in 1837.

The winged winds the messengers of our way.
Our father wished, and might have urged our stay:
But when the loud and iron sound
Of strokes on strokes, in quick rebound,
Filled with its echoes dread our caves,
In pity, then, without delay,
We cast our maiden blushes far away,
And with unsandaled feet sprung upward from the waves.

    Pro. Wo, wo ! unutterable wo ! Look on me,
Ye sister-nymphs ! children of fruitful Thetis !
Look on me, daughters of Oceanus,
Who rolls his ever-restless stream around
The immeasurable earth: behold me ! see,
In what a coil of endless misery wrapt,
And riveted to this storm-beaten crag,
I keep unenviable watch.

    Cho.   Prometheus !
Well do I see thee, and a cloud of sorrow, [21]
With tears unshed, heavily laden, fills
My eyes to overflowing, thus to see thee
Wasting by slow degrees away, in iron
Adamantean-proof; what room for wonder !
New masters and new laws govern Olympus –
Laws sanctioned by the tyranny of Jove;
And all that once was venerable in heaven
Is held no more in honour.

    Pro. Oh, that I were sunk deep beneath the earth ! [22]

---

[21] 1832: *horror for sorrow.*

[22] 1832: *Oh ! would that I were deep under the earth !*

And in the interminable realms, that hold
The innumerable dead ! impaled, and bound
With heavier chains, if any can be worse,
So that nor god, nor slave of god should laugh
At what I bear: but now I am the sport
Of all the winds of heaven – the scorn and gaze
Of my enemies . . . . . [23]

    Cho.   Alas !
Which of the deities is so hard of heart
As to exult over these agonies?
Save Jove alone, who pities not thine ills?
But he, inflexible of purpose – he,
Uncompassionate, prone to anger, rules
The heavenly race with most despotic sway;
Nor will he cease to tyrannise [24]
Till sated his obdurate soul,
Or till shall come the hour when some revolt,
Or covert guile, may hurl him from his throne;
But how, or when, I cannot guess, so hard
It were in thought to shake his firm-set power.

    Pro. And yet the time will come when, chained
And tortured as thou seest me here, this king
Of heaven, with all his majesty, shall seek
New councils in the impending hour
Of danger to his power and throne:

---

[23] 1832:
   So that nor God, nor any one should exult
   At what I bear, or have to bear; but now,
   I am the sport of all the winds of Heaven,
   The scorn and gaze of my enemies.

[24] 1832: tyrannize.

Then let him try to flatter, and cajole me
With honey-tongued persuasion's incantations,
Or shake my fortitude with threats – alike
Shall be to me his menaces and prayers;
For neither shall avail him, till he loose
These cruel bonds, until he make amends, [25]
And amplest reparation for my wrongs.

 Cho. Thou art invincible in thy fortitude,
And nothing bowest under the stern yoke
Of thy calamity, and thy very words
Are free and daring as thy spirit, that spurns
The bonds that chain its tenement; but I shrink
With horror, from the dread alone
That these thine agonies may have no end.
Where shall thy shattered fortunes find a port?
For inaccessible is the son of Saturn,
And has a most inexorable heart.

 Pro. Such as he is, and making his stern will
Ever his law, I tell thee, this proud despot
Shall be all soft compassion on the day
When this shall come to pass, as come it must,
When this shall set a curb upon his obstinate wrath, [26]
And court my favour; nor shall I be loth
To meet his wish – be reconciled with him.

 Cho. But, come ! your hapless story tell, and say [27]
In what transgression taken, Jove has doomed you,

---

[25] 1832: These cruel cruel bonds, and make amends,

[26] 1832: Shall set a curb upon his obstinate wrath,

[27] 1832: But come ! tell all your hapless story, say !

Thus trampled, thus expelled, to suffer these
Most ignominious and unseemly torments?
But do not tell it, if your words afflict you.
    Pro. Hard is the task for me to speak these things,
And painful is the effort to be silent –
Nothing is left me now but misery !
Need I repeat, what anarchy arose
Among the gods, when each opposed to each,
Stirred up revolt in heaven, aspiring some
To hurl down Saturn from his ancient throne,
That Jove might reign, and some as fiercely urging
That he should never hold dominion there?
Then I, consulting for the best, had hoped
To move the Titans; but those sons of Earth [28]
And Uranus, setting me at naught, and all
Prudent designs, in their proud hearts conspired
To put his high supremacy to the proof,
By dint of force, and bold rebellion – hoping
Thus to obtain the monarchy of the gods.
Too well I knew the issue of that fight:
Not only from my own foreknowledge, but
Themis, and mother Earth, who bear one shape
In many different names, the same predicted, [29]
That stratagem and guile, not open war,
Or strength of arms, should gain the rule in heaven.

---

[28] 1832: *earth* in lower case.

[29] 1832:
    Not from my own foreknowledge, nor alone
    From Themis, but my mother Earth, one shape
    In many names, not once, but oft predicted,

This with all arguments due I pressed; but they
Did little deign to look to the to-come.
Which when perceived, and weighing well the event,
My mother and myself – I nothing loth,
And she all willing – reinforced the ranks
Of Jove. Then, too, he was all gratitude:
And thus, upheld by us and by our joint arms, [30]
And by my counsels, Saturn old was plunged,
With the companions of his overthrow,
Down to the bottomless pit of Tartarus,
To dwell in utter darkness. Such the good
I did the Omnipotent; and, in return,
Behold how I am recompensed – with evil !
But 'tis a malady innate in tyrants
Never to trust their friends. What need to seek
A stronger ground of hate? Yet ground there was.
Scarce was he seated on his father's throne,
When straight, to strengthen and confirm his power,
He shared among his gods, and gave to each
A separate attribute. But for hapless mortals
Reserved he none: them he the rather thought
At once to annihilate, creating some
New race of beings. His designs, save me,
None of the inhabitants of heaven opposed.
I stood between his wrath and man, lest he

---

[30] 1832:
And she as willing, reinforced Jove's ranks;
Then too he was all gratitude, and thus
Upheld by us and by our conjoint arms,

Should fall into perdition, and go down [31]
In misery to the grave ..... thus interceding .....
See with what penal agonies I am bowed down!
Dreadful to bear! and pitiable to behold!
Pity was my sole crime. Did I for this
Deserve that, pitilessly singled out
From all, I should be made a spectacle,
Affording little glory to high Jove?

   Cho. He must be made of adamant and flint,
Who would not pity thy calamities.
Would I had not beheld them – but, beholding,
My heart bleeds for thee!

   Pro.   Even to my foes
I were a pitiable sight. [32]

   Cho.   But say!
Did you not go beyond what you confess?

   Pro. I taught mankind that they should not die daily,
Have death before their eyes – the fear of death.

   Cho. What remedy didst thou find for this disease?

   Pro. I made blind hopes the inmates of their breasts. [33]

   Cho. This was, indeed, a mighty boon to man!

---

[31] 1832:
   New race of beings like to man ..... then none,
   Of all the inhabitants of heaven, opposed,
   Or dared oppose his will, save one alone .....
   I stood between his wrath and them, lest they
   Should fall into perdition, going down

[32] 1832:
                To my friends indeed
  I am a pitiable sight!

[33] 1832: I made blind hopes the inhabitants of their breasts.

Pro. Nay, more, I brought them fire.
   Cho.   The ephemeral things !
Have they the ruddy flame?
   Pro.   By which they may
Learn many useful arts.
   Cho.   And has, for this,
Jove visited you with torments such as these?
Is there no term assigned them?
   Pro.   None, but when
To him it shall seem good.
   Cho.   Fallacious hope !
And is your heart alive to consciousness?
Hast thou no sense of guilt? But how offending,
Ill suits it me to tell, and 'twould be hard [34]
For you to hear; then let me pass it by:
Look for some means to loose your bonds.
   Pro.   'Tis easy
For one whose path of life is free from cares,
And sorrows, to give counsel, and find words
Of much reproof to tax with evil those
Who walk in misery ..... nor can I plead
My ignorance in aught; for willingly,
Willingly I transgressed, nor can deny it;
The penalty that must be paid for man,
I knew in benefiting man ..... but this .....
Ah, no ! I did not dream of pangs like these,

---

[34]1832:
               Seem good to him !
   Fallacious hope ! hast thou no sense of guilt?
   Perceive you not ..... but how thou hast offended,
   It pleases not me to tell, and 'twould be hard

Of such a retribution !..... Was it fit
That in a rugged solitude of rocks
I should eternally abide, and make
This crag's inhospitable gorge my dwelling?
But grieve no more over my present pains.
Forsake your car – alight, that you may learn
All that has yet befallen, or may befall me,
Unto the end: yield to my earnest prayer,
And give your fellowship of wo to one
Who now needs most the interchange of souls [35]
In sympathy. For ever on the wing
Does adverse fortune shift from place to place,
And flit from one to another. [36]
    Cho.   We have heard,
Nor have you urged in vain your prayer;
And now behold us reconciled
With ready foot to quit our swift-plumed car,
Exchanging for the realms of the pure air,
The trackless pathway of the bird,
This precipice on precipices piled.
Prometheus, we will listen to thy woes,
And hear them o'er and o'er, to this their close !

Enter OCEANUS.

    Oce. Borne on the pinions strong of my fleet bird,
Who knows instinctively my will, and needs

---

[35] 1832: Who needs it most; like interchange of souls

[36] 1832: From one fly to another.

No rein to guide, a long and difficult way
Measuring, through fields of boundless space, I come
To mourn with thee, Prometheus; for the ties
Of kindred blood prevailed, and led me on
Desirous to behold thee – sympathise [37]
In all that thou endurest: and were I
Other than of your kindred, not the less
Wouldest thou share my pity or regard.
Trust, then, in all I say; for I am one
Of those who hate the flattering gloss of words.
If aught in my ability may serve
To lighten thine affliction, now declare it;
For never shalt thou say thou hadst a friend
More true to thee than is Oceanus.
    Pro. It may be so. What! and art thou too come
To be spectator of my miseries?
Couldst thou prevail upon thyself to leave
The floods that take thy name, thy rock-roofed caves,
The work of nature's hand, to visit this
Inhospitable realm, that bears but iron?
And art thou come to look on my afflictions,
Compassionate my sufferings? Thou seest
A spectacle might well excite thy pity, –
A god, the friend of Jove, who fought for Jove,
Stood by him, placed him on his throne, weighed down
With chains – ye need not ask by whom! [38]
    Oce.   Too well,

---

[37] 1832: Desirous to behold thee, and take part

[38] 1832: ye for you.

Prometheus, do I see thee ! and desire
To aid thee with best counsels, though thou art
Various in counsel. Know thyself, for thou
Knowest his power: then put on a new mind,
For a new monarch lords it o'er the gods.
And if such sharp and barbed words thou slingest
Against Jove's majesty, beware lest he,
High-throned above the highest, where he sits
In distance unapproachable, may hear,
And in his anger make the ills you have
Seem mere child's play to those he may inflict. [39]
Are you not miserable enough, that you
Must cherish impotent ire? Oh, seek some means
To reconcile yourself with him ! . . . . . Perhaps
My words seem but the dotage of old age,
As arrogant tongues, in their excess of pride,
Are used to style them, oft their sole reward:
Nor are you of the humblest; or you long since
Had bowed to your inevitable lot.
What would you? Pile upon the ills you have
Other and greater ills ! Let me, then, move you !
Yield to me ! take me for your guide and counsellor,
Nor longer kick against the pricks; a monarch [40]
Implacable, uncontrolled, is he who reigns.
And now I go, striving, if so I may
Gain your deliverance: and do you, meantime,
Set watch upon your lips, and guard them well

---

[39] 1832: boyish tasks for mere child's play.

[40] 1832: spurs for pricks.

From daring speech. And have you now to learn,
With all your wisdom, that a foolish tongue,
And given to vanity, works its own bane?

    Pro. I gratulate you, confederate as you were,
And all-acquainted with my daring thoughts,
That they worked you no bane. But leave me now!
Nor waste a thought or care on me! In vain
Would you persuade him, for he is a god
That may not be entreated; and take heed
You meet yourself no injury by the way.

    Oce. Wise as your counsels are, it would appear,
As facts not words best argue, that they serve
To benefit yourself less than your friends.
But me you will not from my purpose turn,
Urge what thou mayest; I glory in the boast –
I boast, I say, that to my mediation
Great Jove will listen, free you from these bonds.

    Pro. Oceanus! I feel your proffered kindness,
Nor shall I cease to own, that in good will
You yield to none: but labour not in vain
To do me service, for you will but lose
Your labour, nothing benefiting me.
Thou keep aloof, and look to your own safety.
Great as my sufferings are, I would not wish
That any, the least portion of my woes,
Should fall on others. Take no thought of me!
Nor grieve I solely for my own misfortunes,
But keenest anguish racks me for my brother,
Atlas, who, in the country of the west
Stands, like a column, on his shoulders bearing,
Immoveably suspended, Heaven and Earth,

A burthen scarce imaginable; nay, more,
That son of Earth! the dweller of the caves
Cilician ! I did pity to behold:
Immeasurable monster! And could not
Thy hundred heads, Typhon ! avail thee? nor
Thy jaws, whose hiss was death; and Gorgon eyes,
Whose terrors flashed devouring flames, had they
No might to shake the sovereignty of heaven? –
No! him the sleepless thunder-bolt of Jove,
Winged with red lightning and combustion dire,
Confounded, vanquished, blasted, soul-subdued;
And now his strength-abandoned corse, outstretched
For many a rood, lies near the narrow sea,
Under the roots of Etna, on whose peaks
Vulcan oft sits, hammering the ardent mass,
Whence rivers of liquid fire shall burst forth, [41]
To ravage with fierce waves the lovely fields
Of fruitful Sicily: for even now
Does Typhon, boiling with indignant wrath,
From out the gulf of torture where he lies,
Prepare to spout forth globes on globes of fire,
As in defiance of Jove's thunder still.
Not inexperienced in the ills of others,
You need not look to me as an instructor;
Make, then, your knowledge useful to yourself:
And I, as best I may, will bear the lot
I have, till Jove shall intermit his vengeance.
    Oce. Dost thou not know, that words are sweet physicians
To minds diseased with wrath?

---

[41]1832: Whence shall burst forth rivers of liquid fire,

Pro.   By timely means,
And slow degrees, a remedy should be sought;
But violence must aggravate the wound
In bosoms fevered with revenge.
   Oce.   Then tell me!
What harm can nerve combined with caution bring?
   Pro. Superfluous labour, and a rash benevolence.
   Oce. Suffer me to prescribe for your disease:
It profits oft the wise to doubt their wisdom.
   Pro. Learn that from me, this deed will pass for mine.
   Oce. You force me to return then!
   Pro.   I would not
Pity for me should bring you into thrall.
   Oce. Speak you of him just seated on heaven's throne—
The Omnipotent?
   Pro.   Doubt it not: beware of him,
Lest his heart ache[42] with wrath.
   Oce.   Your fate, Prometheus,
Serves as a lesson to the wise.
   Pro.   Depart!
Begone! and keep the mind you have.
   Oce.   I go!
Nor need more words; my fleet four-footed bird
Flaps with broad plumes the liquid waste of air,
Impatient in his much-loved lodge to bend
His knees beneath his wing.

---

[42] Spelled *ake* in 1832, *ach* in 1837 - here changed to the current spelling, *ache*.

CHORUS. PROMOTHEUS.

CHORUS. — MONOSTROPHE.

Prometheus ! victim of immortal hate !
I mourn for thee, and for thy fate.
And from my pity-streaming eyes,
    To wet my cheek with an exhaustless river,
Do fountain-springs of tears arise,
    And flow ..... and must flow on for ever .....
The sovereign will decreed for thee
    An evil lot, in evil hour,
A most funereal destiny;
    And in the greatness of his power
Make Gods, whom he supplanted, feel
The keen edge of his tyrant steel:
I mourn for thee, and for thy fate,
Thou victim of immortal hate !

STROPHE.

And with its echoes all the region round,
    In harrowing accents, tells thy tale,
    Joins in a sadly lengthened wail,
Sets up a doleful sound.
    With one accord they weep for thee
And the gone glories of thy state:
Of thee and thine, proud, old, and great,
    They mourn the destiny;
Thee all the mortal race, who dwell
    In Asia's venerable seat,

Lament – and thou dost merit well
   The voice of wail they all repeat:
They mourn for thee, and for thy fate,
Thou victim of immortal hate !

ANTISTROPHE.

Thee mourn the dwellers of the Colchian land,
   The fearless virgins who delight
   To mingle in the din of fight;
And thee, the Scythian band.
   Thee, too, Chalybia's flower and pride, [43]
A bold and hardy mountain race,
Who in their fortress, at the base
   Of Caucasus, abide,
And poise the spear, the javelin shake,
   Through all the tract of mountains near
The shores of the Mœotic lake,
   Lament; their voice of wail I hear:
They mourn for thee, and for thy fate,
Thou victim of immortal hate !

EPODE.

Save one, the Titan Atlas, whom with thee
Shall I compare in misery,
   Or match in fate?
He, racked with never-ending pains,
And bound in adamantine chains,

---

[43] 1832: *Arabia's* for *Chalybia's*.

Earth and the vault of heaven sustains –
>An unimaginable weight.
>>The surges of the ocean,
>>In undulating motion,
To thy perpetual wail accordance keep.
Responsive wails the lowest deep;
And in a lower deep unfathomable,
>Beneath the seas, beneath earth's seats,
Through all its black abysses, Hell,
>With many a voice, one moan repeats;
Rivers, and all the fountains as they flow,
In murmurs tell their wo:
They mourn for thee, and for thy fate,
Thou victim of immortal hate !

Pro. Deem not that pleasure in your words, or pride,
Have kept me thus long silent; deep and painful
Have been the workings of my soul, to look
Upon myself, my ignominy, and shame .....
To whom do all my late compeers owe all
The gifts and attributes of gods they have,
But me? ..... yet why repeat this tale to you .....
Who know that which I was ..... see what I am .....
First learn the catalogue of my benefits
To mortals ..... how I found them like to brutes,
And filled them with intelligence and reason;
Think not I would accuse mankind, or blame:
I say this but to shew[44] you how I loved them.
For they had eyes, and yet they saw not; ears

---

[44]In 1832: show.

Had they, and they did not hear; but like
Disjointed images in dreams, that have
No order or connexion, they beheld
In the distorted reflex of their vain
Imaginations, all things . . . . . not as now
Did they build houses, to let in the light
And warmth; they had no works of wood or stone,
But underneath the ground in dismal cells, [45]
And sun-unvisited caves, resembling more
The mansions of the dead than dwellings fit
For man and living beings, they abode
Like hoarding ants . . . . . nor had they certain signs
By which to mark the seasons and their change,
Winter, and spring, odorous with breath of flowers,
And summer with its plenteousness of fruits:
No thought but of the present, they lived on
From day to day, improvident, till through me
They learnt the courses of the stars, and knew
Their rising and their setting – difficult science,
And unattainable by time, or toil,
Or unassisted meditation. . . . . . next,
Numbers – inestimable prize ! – I gave;
And that surpassing knowledge, to combine
Symbols and characters, to serve for speech;
And, more than all, at last came Memory,

---

[45] In 1832:
All things in the distorted mirror of
Their vain imaginations ..... not as now,
They built them houses, to let in the beams
Of light, and warmth, they had no works of wood,
Or stone, but underneath the ground, in cells,

Teacher of every art, mother of song.
Who led the ox, and bowed him to the yoke?
And gave man beasts of burthen, to support
The heaviest of his toils? Who tamed the horse
To draw the chariot, and, with willing rein,
To serve the superfluity of wealth?
'Twas I. None other than myself first made [46]
The bark, and sails with bird-like wings outspread,
To bear the wandering mariner o'er the deep.
Wretch that I am! so provident for others,
I can with all my skill devise no means
Of piloting myself.

    Cho.   Shameful your pangs!
And your mind wanders in a maze of error;
And like a bad physician, seized with some
Deep malady, you despond, and find no cure
To medicate yourself.

    Pro.   Yet hear me still;
And, hearing, you will wonder more and more
At all the benefits I heaped on mortals. [47]
What blessing could be greater than the art,
Teaching them, by the secret force of nature,
The potent influences of herbs and plants
To medicine all diseases? For, till then,
Such was their utter ignorance, that, if ta'en [48]
With any malady, there was known no aid

---

[46] 1832: Say, too! did other than myself invent

[47] 1832: conferred for heaped.

[48] 1832: taken for ta'en.

Of potion, food, or unguent: so they pined
In irremediable pangs, and died
In hopeless misery . . . . . divination, then,
And its mysterious agency, I unveiled;
And taught man, with all-penetrating eye,
From dreams and visions of the night to read
Futurity, and separate the false from true
Portents, and signs, and symbols, and the power
Of omen and of augury, from the flight
Of taloned dwellers of the air, their lives,
Their animosities, and fondnesses,
Their pairing and their brooding times; nor less
Of sacrifice, from victims on the shrine –
Till then a wonder and a mystery –
Did I interpret and explain: but, chief
Of all, unequalled presents, brass and iron,
Silver and golden ore, hid in the ground,
Who shall pretend he gave to man but me?
If such there be, know that he idly boasts.
In one brief sentence sum, then, up this truth –
All useful arts on earth sprung from Prometheus!
    Cho. For mortals care no more; to your own loss
Already hast thou benefited man:
Think of your miserable self, and I
Still breathe a hope, that, from your bondage freed,
You yet may one day live a life like Jove's
    Pro. Not till weighed down with misery to the dust,
And full of ills and wrongs, does fate decree –
Fate that brings all things to an end, that I
Shall 'scape these chains: all art and wisdom yield
To stern necessity.

Cho.   All?
Pro.   Ay, all ! save
The triple Fates, and unforgiving Furies.
    Cho. And Jove ! yields he to them?
    Pro.   Even Jove himself
Cannot avoid his destiny.
    Cho.   Say'st thou?
What destiny is Jove's, but to reign on
Through all eternity?
    Pro.   Question me no more !
Further inquiry will avail you naught.
    Cho. It must be some great mystery you would hide.
    Pro. It is a secret – must be kept with care.
Scarce dare I breathe it to myself; for, locked
Within my heart's recesses, I, through it,
May one day haply end this shameful bondage.

CHORUS. – STROPHE.

O Thou ! the incomprehensible
    Ruler of all ! be far the hour,
    When thou may'st set thy sovereign power
Against my feeble will:
    But ever, near my father's flood,
    By many an offered victim's blood,
May I live on, to deprecate
The gods, their vengeance, and their hate.
Let this, my fervent prayer, be heard –
Oh, may I never sin in word !
Turn thou my thoughts and steps from ill,
And keep, oh ! keep me in allegiance still !

ANTISTROPHE.

He is my trust, and still shall be
    The guiding shepherd of my way –
    The hope that, to my latest day,
Shall still companion be:
    And hope, sweet hope, can soothe and bless
    With peace of mind and gentleness.
But upon thee all woes are piled.
Thou art immortal, yet exiled
From hope, and bound with every ill:
For, guided by thy stubborn will,
Thou would'st not Jove – great Jove – revere, [49]
But didst forsake high Heaven to worship here.

EPODE.

And what is man, that thou hast given
To him the choicest boons of heaven?
Expect you from that reckless race,
Or gratitude, or aid, or praise?
What is the race of mortals? say !
The ephemeral insects of the beam,
The shadowy shapes that people dream,
    And vanish with the day !
    Are not more real than they !
And shall the vain designs of man
Pervert Jove's all-harmonious plan?
These truths I have been taught to see

---

[49] 1832: *Jove's* for *Jove* in both cases.

  In thy funereal fate;
And new the strain of wo to me,
  And different far from that which late
    I sung for thee,
When to your Hymeneal bed,
With nuptial rites and offerings due, you led
  My sister fair, Hesione.

    Io. Prometheus. Chorus

Io. What land is this? what country? – ah ! what race
Of beings these? My eyes misrepresent,
Or I do seem to see another? – Who
Are thou, fixed to these adamantine crags,
That winterest, bleaching in this waste of rocks,
And icy solitudes? Oh, say ! for what
Unequalled crime hast thou been visited
With such unheard-of punishment? ..... speak ! declare
Whither my wretched devious steps have led me?
Ai ! Ai ! once more ! . . . . . yet once again; I feel
The maddening sting ..... it goads me still ! ..... Avaunt !
And quit my sight ! let the earth cover thee !
Thou spectre of the Earth-born Argus ! Hence,
Horrible apparition ! hence ! I shudder
To look on thee, false many-sighted monster !
Cannot the grave hide thee among her dead?
Am I not miserable enough, that thou
Must come again, in all thy living horrors,
To follow me from the dead? Where'er I turn
The vision haunts me, drives me, drags me on,
Weary and faint, and hoping to elude

His steps, pursuing ever along the sands
Of the sea-shore, whilst still the pipe of reeds,
Monotonously tuned, drones in my ear
The self-same drowsy notes . . . . . Alas ! alas !
Where am I? whither have I been? where, where
Have my immeasurable wanderings brought me?
What fault, O son of Saturn ! didst thou find
In me, that thou shouldst yoke me with a weight
Of such unutterable agony,
And drive me to despair and madness? Oh !
Melt me with fire, or bury me in the earth,
Or to the ravening monsters of the deep
Make me a prey ! ..... Grant thou my prayer ! ..... behold,
To what a nakedness of misery
My wanderings have reduced me !
Nor can I guess when they shall find an end.

    Cho. Hear'st thou the voice of one – a maid she seems –
Distorted from the likeness of aught human
By some strange transformation?

    Pro.   Hear I not
The voice of wail? ..... It is the virgin daughter
Of Inachus wrought to frenzy, who enwraps
With love, as with a flame, the heart of Jove,
And now is driven, by Juno's jealous hate,
From land to land, a shelterless exile !

    Io.   Who
Names thus my father? How canst thou know me,
So wretched thou, and I so miserable !
Speak ! answer ! nor deny me; for thy words
Are words of truth, and they do image well
The force of my calamity: for I am

As one urged by a cruel master's will
On some far course, who, as the maddening spur
Sharp goads her side, springs forward with the throes
Of a new agony, at every step
Tottering with hunger, weariness, and pain.
But who could bear, and over-live, like me,
All forms of wretchedness, all extremes of wo?
Yet, if thou canst, I would thou might'st impart
What more I have to suffer, or what do [50]
To cure my ills: in pity speak ! console
A way-worn, lost, forsaken, helpless outcast !

   Pro. I will explain whate'er you wish to know,
In simple language and unvarnished phrase,
And uninvolved in mystery, as friend
Should do to friend. First, then, you see before you
Prometheus, who bestowed on mortals fire.

   Io. Light of the world, that shone to bless mankind !
Hapless Prometheus ! can it be, that thou
Art doomed to suffer thus? For what misdeed?

   Pro. I have but ceased bewailing my sad fate.

   Io. Canst thou not grant a boon to me?

   Pro.   Declare it.
What would'st thou question? say ! To all you ask
I will reply as freely.

   Io.   Tell me, first,
Who chained you to the rock?

   Pro.   The will of Jove,
And hand of Vulcan !

   Io.   But the crime?

---

[50] 1832: What more I have to suffer, what should do?

Pro.   Enough !
Let it suffice thee what thou know'st already.
    Io. But say, what term shall have my wanderings?
    Pro. Better you should remain in ignorance
Than know your fate.
    Io.   Oh ! hide not from me one
Of all my sufferings !
    Pro.   Deem me not discourteous
If I refuse to answer to your prayer.
    Io. Do you still pause to make them known to me?
    Pro. 'Tis that I fear to rack your heart.
    Io.   Fear not !
Nor spare me: think not of my toils –
Bestow no other thought on them than what
It pleases me to do.
    Pro.   Since then perforce
You thus wilt have it, I will speak. Listen ! [51]
    Cho. Stay ! be it ours to share in this sad pleasure.
First hear we from herself her hapless story:
What else may yet betide her you shall teach.
    Pro. Begin, then, Io ! and this grace accord them,
The rather that they are thy father's cousins: [52]
To find an echo for your sighs, and tears
Of tenderest sympathy for those you shed,
This thy reward ..... and it shall well repay thee.
    Io. And must I? How shall I obey you ! Yet,
As plainly as I may, I will relate

---

[51] The preceding 34 lines are missing from the 1832 book.

[52] 1832: *sisters* for *cousins*.

All you would hear. Alas ! to tell the tale,
To look upon my altered self, and say
How fell this storm, raining on me from heaven,
Fills me with shame and anguish ..... In slumbers oft,
Did visioned shapes of night flit round my couch,
And tongues did syllable in accents sweet [53]
These words: "Why dost thou waste thy flower of youth
In lone virginity? Fair though thou art,
Deem thyself greatly favoured above thy sex,
Thrice fortunate child ! The king of gods and men
Has chosen for his bride, and destines thee
For his immortal arms; nor thou disdain
To share his love. Fly, then ! forsake thy couch,
For marshy Lerna's valleys deep, and stalls,
And pastures green, where graze thy father's kine,
That Jove may satisfy his eyes' desire."
Again, and yet again, the vision came,
To break my sleep, and fill my heart with strange
Emotions; till, emboldened by my fears,
All I had seen and heard I told my sire.
Whereon to Delphi, and the sacred groves
Oracular that gird Dodona's shrine, [54]
He sent his seers, consulting how he might,
By word or deed, do aught to please the gods.
At first, the deity replied in sounds

---

[53] 1832:
   Fills me with shame and anguish ..... Oft in sleep,
   Used visioned shapes of night to haunt my couch,
   And tongues to syllable in accents sweet

[54] 1832: Oracular, that crown Dodona's steep,

Of doubtful purport, words of mystery, terms
Of meaning most perplexed: at last there came
An answer, clear and unambiguous – ah !
Too clear – commanding Inachus to send me
From his own hearth and my dear native land,
A wanderer to the furthest bounds of earth,
Lest fire should fall from heaven on him and his,
And utterly exterminate his race:
And he . . . . . believing in the prophecy,
And in obedience to the will of Jove,
– What could he less? alas ! I blame him not –
With heavy heart drove me, with heavier still,
Forth from my home, and shut the door against me.
Oh ! then there came a change upon me – such
A change ! wo's me ! my shape and features grew
Deformed, and hideous as you see; nor was
My mind distorted less, but filled with vain
Imaginations, peopled by the Furies;
Till, with winged speed and desperate bounds, I sought
Cenchrea's crystal stream, and Lerna's marsh, [55]
Where the fell eyes that knew no sleep were sent
To watch my steps, till unexpected fate
Deprived of life the earth-born herdsman, Argus:
While I, to madness stung by scourge divine, [56]
Am driven from land to land. Thou know'st the past,

---

[55] 1832: Cencrea's crystal stream, and Lerna's fount,

[56] 1832:
    To watch my steps: that earth-born herdsman Argus
    An unexpected fate deprived of life:
    And I to madness stung by scourge divine,

And tell me, if thou canst, of what I yet
Must bear; nor with false delicacy, in words [57]
Of studied speech, the shame of wisdom, hide
The truth from hapless Io.

    Cho. Ai! Ai! for thee! Ai! Ai! for thee!
No more! no more! in pity cease!
Never dreamed I of ills like these!
Or that such accents of despair,
So strange, so full of fear,
Should harrow up my soul to hear.
Sad to behold thou art,
And difficult to bear
Thy wanderings, thine injuries, and thy woes:
When shall they close?
At every tone of thine, at every word,
Pity and horror pierce my heart,
As with a two-edged sword,
Ai! Ai! for thee! Ai! Ai! for thee!.....

    Pro. You are too full of fears; you wail too soon:
Wait till you know the rest.

    Io.   Say on! Say on!
'Tis good for those labouring in maladies
To know the pangs they yet may have to prove. [58]

    Pro. My ready wishes furthered your desire
To learn, as well you might, first from herself
Her hapless story; what is yet to come,
The sufferings she must bear from Juno's hate,

---

[57] 1832: May have to bear? nor in false pity, by words

[58] In 1832 these three lines were assigned to the Chorus.

Must now be told: and treasure well my words,
Daughter of Inachus! that you through them
May find a period to your wanderings.
First, then, on turning to the rising sun,
Follow the uncultivated tracts that hold
The Scythian Nomades, distinguished well
By bows and quivered darts, and huts composed
Of twisted osiers, raised on wheels, that bear
The dwellings of those errant tribes: approach
Not them, but skirt their deserts, and incline
Along the sounding cliffs of the sea-shore,
Till on the left you pass the Chalybes
Who forge and temper iron. Avoid their tribe; [59]
They are inhuman and inhospitable.
You come now to the river, rightly named
From its rude boisterous torrent; ford it not:
For 'tis not safely fordable until
You reach the head of Caucasus, that exceeds [60]
In height all mountains, from whose loftiest peaks
That river pours its strength and volume forth.
Those peaks touch heaven, and yet they must be crost.
Thence southward lies your course, till you shall meet
The warlike Amazons, who hate the race
Of man (erewhile to dwell in Themiscyra,
On the Thermodon's banks, whose many mouths

---

[59] 1832: who forge and temper iron, avoid them, for

[60] 1832:
   You come now to the Lixus, rightly named
   From its shrill chiding torrent, ford it not,
   Nor is it safely fordable, until
   You reach the foot of Caucasus, that exceeds

From Salmydessus,[61] step-mother to ships,
Dread of the mariner); not unwilling, they,
For sex is kind to sex, will be your guides. [62]
On journeying still, you will ere long behold
An isthmus, 'twixt whose narrow gates appears
The dark Cimmerian lake: fear not its waves,
But boldly traverse the Mœotic strait;
Whence great shall be the fame among mankind
Of this your daring passage, to be called,
From you, the Bosphorus . . . . . Europe is behind,
And Asia all before . . . . . And now, ye nymphs !
Ask your inquiring minds, if mighty Jove
Can tyrannise o'er all, as well as me —
Question his justice too, that he, a god,
The king of gods, immortal as he is,
To gratify his passion, dooms a mortal,
A helpless maid, to wanderings such as these !

    Prom. Virgin ! thou hast, indeed, a cruel bridegroom
This is no more than prelude to your woes —
The worst remains behind, unheard . . . . . untold. [63]

    Io. Ai ! Ai !

    Pro.   And dost thou too again
Begin to weep and wail? What will you do
When you have heard the whole !

---

[61] 1832: Salmydyssus.

[62] 1832:
  Dread of the mariner,) like women, they
  With willing minds will lead you on your road:

[63] 1832 incorrectly assigns these lines to Io.

Cho.   Has she to hear
Of miseries yet to come?
 Pro.   A stormy ocean !
Waves upon waves of miseries !
 Io.   Alas !
What is there in this being, that I should wish
To cling to it; what can I hope to gain
By living on? Then, let me welcome death !
Cast myself headlong down from this sharp rock
To the far plain, and, dashed below, thus end
At once my woes: better to die at once,
Than suffer all my life the pangs of death.
 Pro. What are your petty griefs compared to mine?
Behold me ! Dost thou think thou could'st endure
The pangs I bear, and live . . . . . but I, alas !
I cannot die, – for death would be a blessing,
Would cure my ills, and therefore must I live;
But they can know no end till falls the tyrant.
 Io. Shall Jove then fall, – he lose his power?
 Pro.   Methinks
You would not grieve to see the day !
 Io.   Not grieve !
I should rejoice ! Do I not wrongfully
Suffer from Jove?
 Pro.   Feeling and suffering thus,
You shall know more.
 Io.   Say, then ! by whom shall fall
The tyrant; who shall rob him of his sceptre?
 Pro. Himself, and the blind passions that enslave him.
 Io. What passions? how ! speak ! if your words offend not.
 Pro. He little dreams of his disastrous marriage !

 Io. Divine, or human, name it if thou darest!
 Pro. How dare? I dare say all. Yet – no.
 Io.   His marriage!.....
Shall a wife shake his throne?
 Pro.   She shall bring forth
A son, who shall be mightier than his father.
 Io. Is there no way he can escape this?
 Pro.   One!
And only one! my freedom from these bonds.
 Io. And who shall set you free against Jove's will?
 Pro. A child of thine! one sprung from thee!
 Io.   Of mine!....
.
A son of mine deliver you from these bonds?
 Pro. To generations three, add ten descents!
 Io. Say on! the prophecy is clouded still!
 Pro. And be it dark – examine it no further,
Nor seek to know what more you have to suffer.
 Io. Let not your proffered kindness be withdrawn
Through any fault of mine.
 Pro.   Take which you will;
You have a double choice.
 Io.   What choice? Explain!
 Pro. Choose! whether shall I tell thee of thyself,
And of thy wanderings, or of him who shall
Be my deliverer.
 Cho.   A double grace
Vouchsafe! and claim a double gratitude!
Impart, what course remains for her, to us
Who shall redeem thee; most I long to know it.
 Pro. I yield to your entreaty, which it ill

Becomes me to oppose; then listen, Io !
And on the tablets of your memory grave
The painful course I have to trace ..... As soon, then, [64]
As you have crossed the pool Mœotis, bound
Of either continent, seek the orient sun,
And meet his burning chariot-wheels; a rough
And boisterous sea o'erpast, you will arrive
At Cisthene's Gorgonian plains, where live
The swanlike maidens three, daughters of Phorcys,
The Grææ; old and wrinkled from their birth,
One eye they have, one tooth, for use of all,
Each in her turn; whom visits not a beam
Of sun by day, or moon by night; and near,
The Gorgons, dragon-winged, and Hydra-tressed,
Those loathsome hags, whose eyes no mortal man
Could look upon, and breathe the breath of life.
I tell you this, to warn you of their power.
Beware, too, of another sight of horror,
The Grypes, Jove's dumb guards, part beast, part bird, [65]
With talons armed, and sharp and crooked beaks;
Nor to be dreaded less, their foes, the troop
Of one-eyed Arimaspians, who abide
About the stream, paven with sands of gold,
Called Pluton; shun with equal care these fiends.
Still onward journeying, you at length shall reach
A sable tribe, whose dwelling is beside
The fountain of the sun, on Niger's banks;

---

[64] 1832: The painful course I have still to trace ..... Soon then,

[65] 1832: The Gryphins, Jove's dumb guards, part-beast, part-bird,

Follow its downward steps, till it descends
A mighty cataract from the Bibline mountains,
And losing there its name of Æthiops,
The sacred Nile with his salubrious tide
Shall lead you on to those deep fertile lands
Whose triple sides his stream encloses, where
A long and numerous colony shall be founded
From you, and from your children, who shall hold
The land in heritage: here end your toils . . . . .
And should you still be doubtful of your way,
Speak ! and I will reply ! fear not to tax
My leisure ! I have more than I could wish.

 Cho. If aught be left unsaid, or unexplained,
Say on ! but should the tale be told, remember
Your promise ! what, I scarcely need remind you.

 Pro. My words have brought her labours to a close;
But, that she may not doubt my narrative,
I will recount, as shortly as I can,
What she endured upon her journey hither;
A certain proof that all I say is true.
First, then, you entered the Molossian plains,
That circuit wide Dodona's grove, the site
Of Jove's Thesprotian shrine, whose sacred oaks
Have gifts prophetic, and from whom you learnt,
Without obscurity, you were doomed to be
The wife of Jove, a flattering fortune truly:
Pursued by furies still, the line of coast
Following, you rushed to Rhea's ample bay,
Whence your reverted steps and devious course
Drifted you hither, know ! in future times,
This deep and inland sea in memory,

And an eternal monument of you,
And of your passage, shall be called Ionian; .....
No more ..... Be this a certain sign, that I
Have a pervading vision, that can pierce
Beyond the narrow bounds of other minds .....
I now return whence I digressed – What yet
Remains, I thus relate to them and you.
There is a city called Canopus, last
Of all that land, built at the mouth of Nile,
And its embankments; Jove will there bring back
Your reason, and restore you to yourself
By his fond touch alone; and named from that
Miraculous pressure of his hand, shall spring
Dusk Epaphus, destined to enjoy the land, [66]
Far as the river with its overflow
Shall irrigate the soil; in line from him
The fifth, two brothers, one with fifty sons, [67]
And one as many daughters, will arise
Which maidens, by their father led, shall fly
To Argos, shunning the detested yoke
Of unpermitted nuptials; but the youths,
Like hawks pursuing madly down the wind
Doves in the eagerness of prey, shall pounce
Upon their kindred, blind to fate, and what
May follow such an ineffectual chase .....
That fate awaits them, in a foreign land,

---

[66] 1832: *Black* for *Dusk*.

[67] 1832:
    Shall irrigate the soil; the fifth in line
    From him, two brothers, one with fifty sons;

Pelasgia hides their bodies, not subdued
In war with men, or vanquished in the day,
But by the hand of virgins, and in darkness,
That nerves the arm to any deeds of blood;
And dark the deed, for each a victim falls
To his wife's dagger on his bridal night:
Such hymeneals light on all my foes !
Yet one shall listen to the voice of love,
And weigh, with woman's mind, the shame of weakness
And infamy of murder, till the soft
And tender pleadings of a passionate heart
Blunt the keen weapon's edge, and save her husband.
In Argos shall she reign, and her son's sons;
But long the tale, and from her race shall spring
The bender of the bow, of force to break
These chains, and end my sufferance . . . . . thus spake,
Oracular, my venerable mother
Titanian Themis; how, and when these things
May come to pass, it boots not me to tell,
Nor would it profit you to hear.

    Io.   Ahi ! Ahi !
Unutterable wo ! Oimé ! Oimé.
I burn ! I burn ! here ! here . . . . . the flame consumes me –
My reason totters on her seat . . . . . the lash
Of furies goads me, the barbed stings of fire
Pierce my heart's core with agony, – my poor heart
In audible pulsation beats against
My breast, and now it stops, – my eyes roll wildly
As bursting from their sockets . . . . . all things spin
In rapid evolution round me, – my brain reels,
As in the whirlwind of my fury torn

I wander from my course . . . . . my tongue denies
Its office, – unconnected ravings all my words !
They cannot image my despair . . . . . my thoughts
O'er whelm and overpower me with their torrent, –
They plunge me deeper in the waves !
And dash me on the rocks ! . . . . . On ! On ! Away !

[Exit Io.]

CHORUS. – STROPHE.

  Beyond all mortal wisdom wise,
     And read in the decrees of fate,
  Was he, who taught 'twas best to prize
     Equality of state, –
  To share content an humble lot
     With one of humble state,
  With wealth or power undazzled not,
     Nor choosing from the great.

ANTISTROPHE.

  This happy lot to me be given;
     I ask but this, to be allied
  With none of all the Gods of Heaven,
     But made an equal bride:
  These thoughts, sad Io ! flow from thee,
     Thou bird without a mate !
  Thou homeless bride, o'er land and sea
     Pursued by jealous hate.

EPODE.

Let all my vows then offered be,
That when I wed, equality
    May bless my nuptial state:
But who a god could see, nor love, –
Ah! who could guard her heart from Jove,
    Or war against her fate?
Unequal would the contest be,
And flying, I should vainly flee
    From beauties all divine.
What is our wisdom to the All-wise,
Our sight but blindness to the eyes
    Of him who dazzled thine?

Pro. Yet all-imperious as he is, and bold,
And arrogant of soul, the day shall come
When his pride shall be humbled and laid low, –
For he shall marry one he should not wed,
Beget a son he should not have begot,
To hurl him from his power, when Saturn's words
Prophetic shall be all-fulfilled, his curse .....
The curses of a father disenthroned
Light on the usurper's head; let him then call
Upon his deities for help; can they
Avert his fate? No! I alone can save him,
The how and when rest but with me: meantime,
Let him enshrined in clouds and darkness trust
In his air-shaking thunders, and rejoice
To vibrate in his hands the forked darts
Of his red lightnings. What shall they avail

In that inevitable hour, when he
Shall fall from his high place of honour – fall
In hideous ruin? for his adversary
Is set up by himself, warring with whom,
He wars against a mightier than himself;
One, who shall find a flame that shall eclipse
The fiercest of his shafts, peals to outroar
Ten thousand of his vollies, and whose bolt
Shall make the trident, with which Neptune shakes
The earth, seem but a spear, and quit his grasp.
When this shall come to pass, then shall he learn
The difference 'twixt the master and the slave.

    Cho. At least you have been free to speak of Jove !

    Pro. Things that shall be consummated, nay, things
I wish to see accomplished.

    Cho.   Dare you paint,
Even to yourself, that day, or him who shall
Subdue great Jove.

    Pro.   The Torturer shall bear
Tortures more difficult to be borne than mine.

    Cho. How ! fear you not to utter words like these?

    Pro. What can I fear, whose destiny it is
Never to die?

    Cho.   Should you provoke his power,
Some stronger, some worse way his wrath may find
To your destruction.

    Pro.   Let him, if he will;
I am prepared to brave it all.

    Cho.   The wise

Do reverence to Nemesis ! [68]
   Pro.   Flatter, cringe,
And worship, let who may be on a throne. [69]
I hold him as the dust beneath my feet;
Do thy worst, tyrant ! yet a little while,
Rule as thou mayst, thou hast not long to reign;
But I behold the runner-slave of Jove,
The ready minister of the new despot: [70]
He comes, no doubt, announcing some fresh outrage.

                Enter MERCURY.

      MERCURY. PROMETHEUS. CHORUS.

   Mer. Thou wise one ! thou in bitterness of tongue
Bitterer than gall ! thou sinner 'gainst the gods ! [71]
And lavisher of their gifts to mortals ! thou
Thief of heaven's fire ! thee I address ! my father
Commands you quickly to reveal what marriage
Thou vainly boast'st may put his throne in danger.

---

[68] 1832: Reverence Nemesis !

[69] 1832:
                        Flatter, cringe those who will,
  In servile adoration at his throne !

[70] 1832:
  But I behold the confidant of Jove,
  The minister, and slave of the new despot,

[71] 1832:
  Thou sophist ! thou in bitterness of tongue
  Bitterer than gall ! thou sinner against the Gods !

Speak ! and without enigmas ! Come ! declare
All that you know; propound it not in terms
Of double meaning: such expedients Jove
Brooks not, not are they fit to soothe his wrath.

   Pro. You come with arrogant address, and words
High-sounding, such as fit the sent and sender.
New masters lord it well: and dost thou deem
The towers of heaven impregnable; have not I
Already seen two tyrants fall? the third
Yet sits upon his throne; his reign shall be
Shorter, his fate more signal far than theirs,
More ignominious ..... haply you may think
I pay not reverence to your new gods,
Or fear them as I ought; and well you may,
Who have gained every thing, – I say not how .....
Whilst I have lost ..... much ..... all I had ..... pursue
The course which led you on to what you are.
And now, tread back your steps to him who sent you:
You will hear nothing that you wish from me.

   Mer. See ! where thine obstinate course has left thee, on
The shoals and quicksands of adversity !

   Pro. Such as I am, know ! I would not exchange
Your slavery for my bonds; better it were
To hug these rocks, and chains, than dog-like live [72]
The passive instrument to such a father.
Thus do I pay you back your taunt !

   Mer.   It seems
You take a pleasure in the abode you have.

   Pro. A pleasure ! ..... would that I could see my foes

---

[72] 1832: To keep these rocks, and chains, than to be made

Thus pleased, and you ..... ay! you, among them.
    Mer.   Me!
What part took I in your misfortunes?
    Pro.   Once
For all, I tell you I hate all the gods,
Who paid me evil, in exchange for good.
    Mer. Your ravings are a madman's, and a part
Of your disease.
    Pro.   If hatred of my foes
Be a sure proof of that disease, I am one.
    Mer. Were you in power, who could brook your pride?
    Pro. Ai me![73]
    Mer. Jove has not learnt such words!
    Pro. But time itself grows old, and teaches all things.
    Mer. Verily, as yet it has not taught you wisdom.
    Pro. Thou has said well, I am not over-wise,
To waste my words upon a slave like thee.
    Mer. Make them more useful, then, and speak to that
My father wants to learn.
    Pro.   In truth I owe
Jove much, and therefore has he sent to me
For a return.
    Mer.   You taunt me like a child!
    Pro. And are you not one; are you not more simple
Than a mere child, dreaming thou can'st persuade
And influence my will? ..... there is no outrage,
Torment, or artifice of Jove, that can
Alter my firm resolve; never will I
Dispense my knowledge, till he loose these chains.

---

[73] 1832: Ahi me! Ahi me!

Then let him hurl his lightnings as he will,
And shake the solid earth with all his thunders,
Pour down a hurricane of white-winged snows,
To sweep resistless ruin, and confound
And mingle all things; me he shall not move,
Nor shake my purpose to reveal by whom
Shall fall the tyrant's sceptre. [74]
    Mer.   But consider,
Before it be too late, if words like these
Can profit you.
    Pro.   I have . . . . . and well . . . . . and long ago
Considered.
    Mer.   Dare ! tongue-valiant ! as you are, [75]
Dare, and for once, in such an ocean tost
And buffeted, to give yourself good counsel.
    Pro. Your words are like the waves upon a rock,
That strike, but move it not: never ! no never [76]
Think, even for a moment, that the fear
Of Jove and all his vengeance can inflict
Shall make me change my nature, or consent,
With hands uplift in womanish supplication,
To deprecate his anger, or court one
Whom I abhor so utterly, – far from me
Be such a thought !

---

[74] 1832:
   Nor shake my purpose never to reveal
   By whom shall fall the tyrant.

[75] 1832: Dare ! tongue-doughty ! as you are,

[76] 1832: That sound, but shake it not: never ! no never

Mer.   　　　　I yet have much to say,
Though haply all I say will be in vain, –
For you are neither softened by entreaties,
Nor moved by prayers, but as an unbroke colt,
Champing the bit, resists with all his force,
And fights against the rein, thus does your fierce
And untamed soul, stubbornly scorn advice: [77]
A pertinacity of thought in one
Who thinks unwisely is not strength, but weakness.
I warn you, then, if obstinately still
You spurn my words, what a tempestuous sea
Of waves inevitably heaped on waves
Of ills shall overwhelm you; first, my sire
Shall tear from its foundations, with his bolt
Of thunder split this rugged crag, and, pent
In its cleft bosom, hurl you with its mass
Down an unfathomable abyss . . . . . to fall . . . . .
And fall, a measureless space of time, till you
Come back to light; and when Jove's winged hound,
The blood-delighting vulture, shall be sent
To tear your body piecemeal, and to glut
His ravenous maw by preying on your vitals,
Shall come, your daily uninvited guest,
To batten on your liver, still renewed,
And black with many a wound of his fell beak,
Insatiate still . . . . . nor look for any term
To these calamities, until some god
Appear to take their weight upon himself,
Piercing the gloomy realms of night and Hades,

---

[77] 1832: And untamed soul, stubborn and weak of counsel:

To seek you in the depths of Tartarus.
Deliberate, then ! these are no idle threats;
But all shall be accomplished as I say:
Jove's will is fate ..... He cannot utter falsehood,
Nor vain one word that cometh from his mouth.
Look round you, and deliberate; nor let
An obstinate perverseness blind thy judgment.
  Cho. It seems to us that Mercury counsels well,
And argues prudently: be not too proud
To listen to his reasonings ..... shame it were
The wise should err in judgment.
  Pro.   Well I knew
The purport of his message, now declared;
'Tis such a one as foe might send to foe;
The torture well becomes the torturer !
Then let him wreak his utmost hate on me,
Loose all his stores of wrath, – on me be thrown
The lightning's arrow, and the balls of fire;
And let the thunder-smoke, and the fierce strife
Of winds warring with winds convulse the air,
Until its breath, with horrible concussion,
Shall tear the firm-set groundsel of the world
Up from its roots, whirl the mad ocean-wave,
With its vexed surges, from their boiling vortex,
To the star-paven vault of heaven; whilst I,
Caught in necessity's irresistible stress,
Am borne aloft awhile, and then dashed down
To the dark gulf of gloomy Tartarus; still
He shall not all-destroy me !
  Mer.   These are but
The intemperate words and ravings wild of madness:

Is he not mad? what wants he of the maniac?
Nay, e'en the best of fortunes would but make
His malady more mortal . . . . . but do you,
Who soothe a portion of his woes, take heed
That ye share not his punishment: go, then,
And quickly, from this place, lest the loud crash
Of unimaginable thunders make
Your reason totter too.
    Cho.   What dost thou say?
Try other . . . . . better counsels, – for to these
Thou never shalt persuade me . . . . . and dost thou
Advise a deed of such dishonour, shame
Your divine nature by such words as those?
Then know me better, know! if such Jove's will,
That what he suffers I will suffer too, –
For I have ever taught myself to hate
Those who forsake their friends; there is no pest
Which I more deprecate and abhor than this.
    Mer. Then bear in mind, that you have been forewarned,
Nor hunting for adversity, tax fortune,
Saying, that Jove has visited you unawares
With this calamity; when knowingly,
And openly, and deliberately, you have laid
A snare to catch yourselves, and taken once,
You'll find it difficult to break the net. [78]
               [Exit MERCURY.]

    Pro. In deed, and not in word – it comes – the earth
Trembles, and shakes, and totters, as convulsed

---

[78] 1832 assigns these seven lines to the Chorus.

With throes of agony; the sullen roar
Of thunder after thunder howls around
In echoes deep, and deepening, flash on flash,
Each fiercer than the last, glares the forked lightning;
The hurricane's wings upbear the volumned dust,
In eddying columns whirl'd – together rush
From every quarter of the heavens, and meet
In ruinous assault the rebel winds,
Making wild anarchy; sky and sea are mingling !
This chaos of all nature has been sent
To shake my soul – rage on, ye elements !
Mother of all my adoration, Earth !
Ether ! who pourest the effluence of light
Round all things, thou who penetratest all things,
Look on my injuries ! see what I suffer. [79]

---

[79] 1832 assigns these seventeen lines to the Chorus.

PROMETHEUS UNBOUND.
By Percy Bysshe Shelley

A LYRICAL DRAMA IN FOUR ACTS.

AUDISNE HÆC AMPHIARAE, SUB TERRAM ABDITE?[1]

SHELLEY'S PREFACE.

The Greek tragic writers, in selecting as their subject any portion of their national history or mythology, employed in their treatment of it a certain arbitrary discretion. They by no means conceived themselves bound to adhere to the common interpretation or to imitate in story as in title their rivals and predecessors. Such a system would have amounted to a resignation of those claims to preference over their competitors which incited the composition. The Agamemnonian story was exhibited on the Athenian theatre with as many variations as dramas.

    I have presumed to employ a similar license. The "Prometheus Unbound" of Æschylus supposed the reconciliation of Jupiter with his victim as the price of the disclosure of the danger threatened to his empire by the consummation of his marriage with Thetis. Thetis, according to this view of the subject, was given in marriage to Peleus,

---

[1] Do you hear this, Amphiaraus, hidden beneath the earth? The mythical Amphiaraus was swallowed up by the earth.

and Prometheus, by the permission of Jupiter, delivered from his captivity by Hercules. Had I framed my story on this model, I should have done no more than have attempted to restore the lost drama of Æschylus; an ambition which, if my preference to this mode of treating the subject had incited me to cherish, the recollection of the high comparison such an attempt would challenge might well abate. But, in truth, I was averse from a catastrophe so feeble as that of reconciling the Champion with the Oppressor of mankind. The moral interest of the fable, which is so powerfully sustained by the sufferings and endurance of Prometheus, would be annihilated if we could conceive of him as unsaying his high language and quailing before his successful and perfidious adversary. The only imaginary being resembling in any degree Prometheus, is Satan; and Prometheus is, in my judgement, a more poetical character than Satan, because, in addition to courage, and majesty, and firm and patient opposition to omnipotent force, he is susceptible of being described as exempt from the taints of ambition, envy, revenge, and a desire for personal aggrandisement, which, in the Hero of *Paradise Lost*, interfere with the interest. The character of Satan engenders in the mind a pernicious casuistry which leads us to weigh his faults with his wrongs, and to excuse the former because the latter exceed all measure. In the minds of those who consider that magnificent fiction with a religious feeling it engenders something worse. But Prometheus is, as it were, the type of the highest perfection of moral and intellectual nature, impelled by the purest and the truest motives to the best and noblest ends.

This Poem was chiefly written upon the mountainous ruins of the Baths of Caracalla, among the flowery glades, and thickets of odoriferous blossoming trees, which are extended in ever winding labyrinths upon its immense platforms and dizzy arches suspended in the air. The bright blue sky of Rome, and the effect of the vigorous awakening spring in that divinest climate, and the new life with which it drenches the spirits even to intoxication, were the inspiration of this drama.

The imagery which I have employed will be found, in many instances, to have been drawn from the operations of the human mind, or from those external actions by which they are expressed. This is unusual in modern poetry, although Dante and Shakespeare are full of instances of the same kind: Dante indeed more than any other poet, and with greater success. But the Greek poets, as writers to whom no resource of awakening the sympathy of their contemporaries was unknown, were in the habitual use of this power; and it is the study of their works (since a higher merit would probably be denied me) to which I am willing that my readers should impute this singularity.

One word is due in candour to the degree in which the study of contemporary writings may have tinged my composition, for such has been a topic of censure with regard to poems far more popular, and indeed more deservedly popular, than mine. It is impossible that any one who inhabits the same age with such writers as those who stand in the foremost ranks of our own, can conscientiously assure himself that his language and tone of thought may not have been modified by the study of the productions of those extraordinary intellects. It is true, that, not the spirit of their genius, but the forms in which it has manifested itself, are due less to the peculiarities of their own minds than to the peculiarity of the moral and intellectual condition of the minds among which they have been produced. Thus a number of writers possess the form, whilst they want the spirit of those whom, it is alleged, they imitate; because the former is the endow-ment of the age in which they live, and the latter must be the uncommunicated lightning of their own mind.

The peculiar style of intense and comprehensive imagery which distinguishes the modern literature of England has not been, as a general power, the product of the imitation of any particular writer. The mass of capabilities remains at every period materially the same; the circumstances which awaken it to action perpetually change. If England were divided into forty republics, each equal in population and extent to Athens, there is no reason to suppose but that, under institutions not more perfect than those of Athens, each would produce philosophers and poets equal to those who (if we except Shakespeare) have never been surpassed. We owe the great writers of the golden age of our literature to that fervid awakening of the public mind which shook to dust the oldest and most oppressive form of the Christian religion. We owe Milton to the progress and development of the same spirit: the sacred Milton was, let it ever be remembered, a republican, and a bold inquirer into morals and religion. The great writers of our own age are, we have reason to suppose, the companions and forerunners of some unimagined change in our social condition or the opinions which cement it. The cloud of mind is discharging its collected lightning, and the equilibrium between institutions and opinions is now restoring, or is about to be restored.

As to imitation, poetry is a mimetic art. It creates, but it creates by combination and representation. Poetical abstractions are beautiful and new, not because the portions of which they are composed had no previous existence in the mind of man or in nature, but because the whole produced by their combination has some intelligible and beautiful analogy with those sources of emotion and thought, and with the contemporary condition of them: one great poet is a masterpiece of nature which another not only ought to study but must study. He might as wisely and as easily determine that his mind should no longer be the mirror of all that is lovely in the visible universe as exclude from his contemplation the beautiful which exists in the writings of a great contemporary. The pretence of doing it would be a presumption in any but the greatest; the effect, even in him, would be strained, unnatural and ineffectual. A poet is the combined product of such internal powers as modify the nature of others; and of such external influences as excite and sustain these powers; he is not one, but both. Every man's mind is, in this respect, modified by all the objects of nature and art; by every word and every suggestion which he ever admitted to act upon his consciousness; it is the mirror upon which all forms are reflected, and in which they compose one form. Poets, not otherwise than philosophers, painters, sculptors and musicians, are, in one sense, the creators, and, in another, the creations, of their age. From this subjection the loftiest do not escape. There is a similarity between Homer and Hesiod, between Æschylus and Euripides, between Virgil and

Horace, between Dante and Petrarch, between Shakespeare and Fletcher, between Dryden and Pope; each has a generic resemblance under which their specific distinctions are arranged. If this similarity be the result of imitation, I am willing to confess that I have imitated.

Let this opportunity be conceded to me of acknowledging that I have, what a Scotch philosopher characteristically terms, "a passion for reforming the world:" what passion incited him to write and publish his book, he omits to explain. For my part I had rather be damned with Plato and Lord Bacon, than go to Heaven with Paley and Malthus. But it is a mistake to suppose that I dedicate my poetical compositions solely to the direct enforcement of reform, or that I consider them in any degree as containing a reasoned system on the theory of human life. Didactic poetry is my abhorrence; nothing can be equally well expressed in prose that is not tedious and supererogatory in verse. My purpose has hitherto been simply to familiarise the highly refined imagination of the more select classes of poetical readers with beautiful idealisms of moral excellence; aware that until the mind can love, and admire, and trust, and hope, and endure, reasoned principles of moral conduct are seeds cast upon the highway of life which the unconscious passenger tramples into dust, although they would bear the harvest of his happiness. Should I live to accomplish what I purpose, that is, produce a systematical history of what appear to me to be the genuine elements of human society, let not the advocates of injustice and superstition flatter themselves that I should take Æschylus rather than Plato as my model.

The having spoken of myself with unaffected freedom will need little apology with the candid; and let the uncandid consider that they injure me less than their own hearts and minds by misrepresentation. Whatever talents a person may possess to amuse and instruct others, be they ever so inconsiderable, he is yet bound to exert them: if his attempt be ineffectual, let the punishment of an unaccomplished purpose have been sufficient; let none trouble themselves to heap the dust of oblivion upon his efforts; the pile they raise will betray his grave which might otherwise have been unknown.

DRAMATIS PERSONÆ.

PROMETHEUS
DEMOGORGON
JUPITER
THE EARTH
OCEAN
APOLLO
MERCURY
Oceanides: ASIA, PANTHEA, IONE,
HERCULES
THE PHANTASM OF JUPITER
THE SPIRIT OF THE EARTH
THE SPIRIT OF THE MOON
SPIRITS OF THE HOURS
SPIRITS. ECHOES. FAUNS. FURIES.

ACT I

SCENE

A Ravine of Icy Rocks in the Indian Caucasus. PROMETHEUS *is discovered bound to the Precipice.* PANTEA *and* IONE *are seated at his feet. Time, night. During the Scene, morning slowly breaks.*

PROMETHEUS

Monarch of Gods and Dæmons, and all Spirits
But One, who throng those bright and rolling worlds
Which Thou and I alone of living things
Behold with sleepless eyes ! regard this Earth
Made multitudinous with thy slaves, whom thou

Requitest for knee-worship, prayer, and praise,
And toil, and hecatombs of broken hearts,
With fear and self-contempt and barren hope.
Whilst me, who am thy foe, eyeless in hate,
Hast thou made reign and triumph, to thy scorn,   10
O'er mine own misery and thy vain revenge.
Three thousand years of sleep-unsheltered hours,
And moments aye divided by keen pangs
Till they seemed years, torture and solitude,
Scorn and despair, – these are mine empire: –   15
More glorious far than that which thou surveyest
From thine unenvied throne, O Mighty God !
Almighty, had I deigned to share the shame
Of thine ill tyranny, and hung not here
Nailed to this wall of eagle-baffling mountain,   20
Black, wintry, dead, unmeasured; without herb,
Insect, or beast, or shape or sound of life.
Ah me ! alas, pain, pain ever, for ever !

No change, no pause, no hope ! Yet I endure.
I ask the Earth, have not the mountains felt?   25
I ask yon Heaven, the all-beholding Sun,
Has it not seen? The Sea, in storm or calm,
Heaven's ever-changing Shadow, spread below,
Have its deaf waves not heard my agony?
Ah me ! alas, pain, pain ever, for ever !   30

The crawling glaciers pierce me with the spears
Of their moon-freezing crystals; the bright chains
Eat with their burning cold into my bones.
Heaven's wingèd hound, polluting from thy lips

His beak in poison not his own, tears up 35
My heart; and shapeless sights come wandering by,
The ghastly people of the realm of dream,
Mocking me: and the Earthquake-fiends are charged
To wrench the rivets from my quivering wounds
When the rocks split and close again behind: 40
While from their loud abysses howling throng
The genii of the storm, urging the rage
Of whirlwind, and afflict me with keen hail.
And yet to me welcome is day and night,
Whether one breaks the hoar-frost of the morn, 45
Or starry, dim, and slow, the other climbs
The leaden-coloured east; for then they lead
The wingless, crawling hours, one among whom
– As some dark Priest hales the reluctant victim –
Shall drag thee, cruel King, to kiss the blood 50
From these pale feet, which then might trample thee
If they disdained not such a prostrate slave.
Disdain ! Ah, no ! I pity thee. What ruin
Will hunt thee undefended through wide Heaven !
How will thy soul, cloven to its depth with terror, 55
Gape like a hell within ! I speak in grief,
Not exultation, for I hate no more,
As then ere misery made me wise. The curse
Once breathed on thee I would recall. Ye Mountains,
Whose many-voicèd Echoes, through the mist 60
Of cataracts, flung the thunder of that spell !
Ye icy Springs, stagnant with wrinkling frost,
Which vibrated to hear me, and then crept
Shuddering through India ! Thou serenest Air,
Through which the Sun walks burning without beams ! 65

And ye swift Whirlwinds, who on poisèd wings
Hung mute and moveless o'er yon hushed abyss,
As thunder, louder than your own, made rock
The orbèd world! If then my words had power,
Though I am changed so that aught evil wish 70
Is dead within; although no memory be
Of what is hate, let them not lose it now!
What was that curse? for ye all heard me speak.

    FIRST VOICE (*From the Mountains*)
Thrice three hundred thousand years
    O'er the Earthquake's couch we stood: 75
Oft, as men convulsed with fears,
    We trembled in our multitude.

    SECOND VOICE (*From the Springs*)
Thunderbolts had parched our water,
    We had been stained with bitter blood,
And had run mute, 'mid shrieks of slaughter, 80
    Thro' a city and a solitude.

    THIRD VOICE (*From the Air*)
I had clothed, since Earth uprose,
    Its wastes in colours not their own,
And oft had my serene repose
    Been cloven by many a rending groan. 85

    FOURTH VOICE (*From the Whirlwinds*)
We had soared beneath these mountains
    Unresting ages; nor had thunder,
Nor yon volcano's flaming fountains,

Nor any power above or under
Ever made us mute with wonder.   90

           FIRST VOICE
But never bowed our snowy crest
As at the voice of thine unrest.

          SECOND VOICE
Never such a sound before
To the Indian waves we bore.
A pilot asleep on the howling sea   95
Leaped up from the deck in agony,
And heard, and cried, 'Ah, woe is me!'
And died as mad as the wild waves be.

           THIRD VOICE
By such dread words from Earth to Heaven
My still realm was never riven: 100
When its wound was closed, there stood
Darkness o'er the day like blood.

          FOURTH VOICE
And we shrank back: for dreams of ruin
To frozen caves our flight pursuing
Made us keep silence – thus – and thus –   105
Though silence is a hell to us.

           THE EARTH
The tongueless caverns of the craggy hills
Cried, 'Misery!' then; the hollow Heaven replied,
'Misery!' And the Ocean's purple waves,

Climbing the land, howled to the lashing winds,   110
And the pale nations heard it, 'Misery !'

PROMETHEUS

I hear a sound of voices: not the voice
Which I gave forth. Mother, thy sons and thou
Scorn him, without whose all-enduring will
Beneath the fierce omnipotence of Jove,   115
Both they and thou had vanished, like thin mist
Unrolled on the morning wind. Know ye not me,
The Titan? He who made his agony
The barrier to your else all-conquering foe?
Oh, rock-embosomed lawns, and snow-fed streams,   120
Now seen athwart frore vapours, deep below,
Through whose o'ershadowing woods I wandered once
With Asia, drinking life from her loved eyes;
Why scorns the spirit which informs ye, now
To commune with me? me alone, who checked,   125
As one who checks a fiend-drawn charioteer,
The falsehood and the force of him who reigns
Supreme, and with the groans of pining slaves
Fills your dim glens and liquid wildernesses:
Why answer ye not, still? Brethren !

THE EARTH
                        They dare not.   130

PROMETHEUS

Who dares? for I would hear that curse again.
Ha, what an awful whisper rises up !
'Tis scarce like sound: it tingles through the frame

As lightning tingles, hovering ere it strike.
Speak, Spirit! from thine inorganic voice   135
I only know that thou art moving near
And love. How cursed I him?

THE EARTH
               How canst thou hear
Who knowest not the language of the dead?

PROMETHEUS
Thou art a living spirit; speak as they.

THE EARTH
I dare not speak like life, lest Heaven's fell King   140
Should hear, and link me to some wheel of pain
More torturing than the one whereon I roll.
Subtle thou art and good; and though the Gods
Hear not this voice, yet thou art more than God,
Being wise and kind: earnestly hearken now.   145

PROMETHEUS
Obscurely through my brain, like shadows dim,
Sweep awful thoughts, rapid and thick. I feel
Faint, like one mingled in entwining love;
Yet 'tis not pleasure.

THE EARTH
           No, thou canst not hear:
Thou art immortal, and this tongue is known   150
Only to those who die.

PROMETHEUS
              And what art thou,
O, melancholy Voice?

              THE EARTH
              I am the Earth,
Thy mother; she within whose stony veins,
To the last fibre of the loftiest tree
Whose thin leaves trembled in the frozen air,   155
Joy ran, as blood within a living frame,
When thou didst from her bosom, like a cloud
Of glory, arise, a spirit of keen joy!
And at thy voice her pining sons uplifted
Their prostrate brows from the polluting dust,   160
And our almighty Tyrant with fierce dread
Grew pale, until his thunder chained thee here.
Then, see those million worlds which burn and roll
Around us: their inhabitants beheld
My spherèd light wane in wide Heaven; the sea   165
Was lifted by strange tempest, and new fire
From earthquake-rifted mountains of bright snow
Shook its portentous hair beneath Heaven's frown;
Lightning and Inundation vexed the plains;
Blue thistles bloomed in cities; foodless toads   170
Within voluptuous chambers panting crawled:
When Plague had fallen on man, and beast, and worm,
And Famine; and black blight on herb and tree;
And in the corn, and vines, and meadow-grass,
Teemed ineradicable poisonous weeds   175
Draining their growth, for my wan breast was dry
With grief; and the thin air, my breath, was stained

With the contagion of a mother's hate
Breathed on her child's destroyer; ay, I heard
Thy curse, the which, if thou rememberest not,   180
Yet my innumerable seas and streams,
Mountains, and caves, and winds, and yon wide air,
And the inarticulate people of the dead,
Preserve, a treasured spell. We meditate
In secret joy and hope those dreadful words,   185
But dare not speak them.

PROMETHEUS
              Venerable mother!
All else who live and suffer take from thee
Some comfort; flowers, and fruits, and happy sounds,
And love, though fleeting; these may not be mine.
But mine own words, I pray, deny me not.   190

THE EARTH
They shall be told. Ere Babylon was dust,
The Magus Zoroaster, my dead child,
Met his own image walking in the garden.
That apparition, sole of men, he saw.
For know there are two worlds of life and death: 195
One that which thou beholdest; but the other
Is underneath the grave, where do inhabit
The shadows of all forms that think and live
Till death unite them and they part no more;
Dreams and the light imaginings of men,   200
And all that faith creates or love desires,
Terrible, strange, sublime and beauteous shapes.
There thou art, and dost hang, a writhing shade,

'Mid whirlwind-peopled mountains; all the gods
Are there, and all the powers of nameless worlds, 205
Vast, sceptred phantoms; heroes, men, and beasts;
And Demogorgon, a tremendous gloom;
And he, the supreme Tyrant, on his throne
Of burning gold. Son, one of these shall utter
The curse which all remember. Call at will 210
Thine own ghost, or the ghost of Jupiter,
Hades or Typhon, or what mightier Gods
From all-prolific Evil, since thy ruin,
Have sprung, and trampled on my prostrate sons.
Ask, and they must reply: so the revenge 215
Of the Supreme may sweep through vacant shades,
As rainy wind through the abandoned gate
Of a fallen palace.

PROMETHEUS
                    Mother, let not aught
Of that which may be evil, pass again
My lips, or those of aught resembling me. 220
Phantasm of Jupiter, arise, appear!

IONE
My wings are folded o'er mine ears:
    My wings are crossèd o'er mine eyes:
Yet through their silver shade appears,
    And through their lulling plumes arise, 225
A Shape, a throng of sounds;
    May it be no ill to thee
O thou of many wounds!
Near whom, for our sweet sister's sake,

Ever thus we watch and wake.   230

PANTHEA
The sound is of whirlwind underground,
    Earthquake, and fire, and mountains cloven;
The shape is awful like the sound,
    Clothed in dark purple, star-inwoven.
A sceptre of pale gold   235
    To stay steps proud, o'er the slow cloud
His veinèd hand doth hold.
Cruel he looks, but calm and strong,
Like one who does, not suffers wrong.

PHANTASM OF JUPITER
Why have the secret powers of this strange world   240
Driven me, a frail and empty phantom, hither
On direst storms? What unaccustomed sounds
Are hovering on my lips, unlike the voice
With which our pallid race hold ghastly talk
In darkness? And, proud sufferer, who art thou?   245

PROMETHEUS
Tremendous Image, as thou art must be
He whom thou shadowest forth. I am his foe,
The Titan. Speak the words which I would hear,
Although no thought inform thine empty voice.

THE EARTH
Listen! And though your echoes must be mute,   250
Grey mountains, and old woods, and haunted springs,
Prophetic caves, and isle-surrounding streams,

Rejoice to hear what yet ye cannot speak.

PHANTASM
A spirit seizes me and speaks within:
It tears me as fire tears a thunder-cloud. 255

PANTHEA
See, how he lifts his mighty looks, the Heaven
Darkens above.

IONE
He speaks ! O shelter me !

PROMETHEUS
I see the curse on gestures proud and cold,
And looks of firm defiance, and calm hate,
And such despair as mocks itself with smiles, 260
Written as on a scroll: yet speak ! Oh, speak !

PHANTASM
   Fiend, I defy thee ! with a calm, fixed mind,
      All that thou canst inflict I bid thee do;
   Foul Tyrant both of Gods and Humankind,
      One only being shalt thou not subdue. 265
   Rain then thy plagues upon me here,
   Ghastly disease, and frenzying fear;
   And let alternate frost and fire
   Eat into me, and be thine ire
Lightning, and cutting hail, and legioned forms 270
Of furies, driving by upon the wounding storms.

   Ay, do thy worst. Thou art omnipotent.
      O'er all things but thyself I gave thee power,
   And my own will. Be thy swift mischiefs sent
      To blast mankind, from yon ethereal tower.   275
   Let thy malignant spirit move
   In darkness over those I love:
   On me and mine I imprecate
   The utmost torture of thy hate;
And thus devote to sleepless agony,   280
This undeclining head while thou must reign on high.

   But thou, who art the God and Lord: O, thou,
      Who fillest with thy soul this world of woe,
   To whom all things of Earth and Heaven do bow
      In fear and worship: all-prevailing foe !   285
   I curse thee ! let a sufferer's curse
   Clasp thee, his torturer, like remorse;
   Till thine Infinity shall be
   A robe of envenomed agony;
And thine Omnipotence a crown of pain,   290
To cling like burning gold round thy dissolving brain.

   Heap on thy soul, by virtue of this Curse,
      Ill deeds, then be thou damned, beholding good;
   Both infinite as is the universe,
      And thou, and thy self-torturing solitude.   295
   An awful image of calm power
   Though now thou sittest, let the hour
   Come, when thou must appear to be
   That which thou art internally;
And after many a false and fruitless crime   300

    Scorn track thy lagging fall through boundless space
        and time.

PROMETHEUS
Were these my words, O Parent?

THE EARTH
        They were thine.

PROMETHEUS
It doth repent me: words are quick and vain;
Grief for awhile is blind, and so was mine.
I wish no living thing to suffer pain.   305

THE EARTH
  Misery, Oh misery to me,
  That Jove at length should vanquish thee.
  Wail, howl aloud, Land and Sea,
  The Earth's rent heart shall answer ye.
  Howl, Spirits of the living and the dead,   310
  Your refuge, your defence, lies fallen and vanquishèd.

FIRST ECHO
Lies fallen and vanquishèd !

SECOND ECHO
Fallen and vanquishèd !

IONE
Fear not: 'tis but some passing spasm,
  The Titan is unvanquished still.   315

But see, where through the azure chasm
    Of yon forked and snowy hill
Trampling the slant winds on high
    With golden-sandalled feet, that glow
Under plumes of purple dye,   320
Like rose-ensanguined ivory,
    A Shape comes now,
Stretching on high from his right hand
A serpent-cinctured wand.

PANTHEA
'Tis Jove's world-wandering herald, Mercury.   325

IONE
And who are those with hydra tresses
    And iron wings that climb the wind,
Whom the frowning God represses
    Like vapours steaming up behind,
Clanging loud, an endless crowd –   330

PANTHEA
These are Jove's tempest-walking hounds,
Whom he gluts with groans and blood,
When charioted on sulphurous cloud
    He bursts Heaven's bounds.

IONE
Are they now led, from the thin dead   335
On new pangs to be fed?

PANTHEA
The Titan looks as ever, firm, not proud.

FIRST FURY
Ha ! I scent life !

SECOND FURY
Let me but look into his eyes !

THIRD FURY
The hope of torturing him smells like a heap
Of corpses, to a death-bird after battle.   340

FIRST FURY
Darest thou delay, O Herald ! take cheer, Hounds
Of Hell: what if the Son of Maia soon
Should make us food and sport – who can please long
The Omnipotent?

MERCURY
          Back to your towers of iron,
And gnash, beside the streams of fire and wail,   345
Your foodless teeth. Geryon, arise ! and Gorgon,
Chimaera, and thou Sphinx, subtlest of fiends
Who ministered to Thebes Heaven's poisoned wine,
Unnatural love, and more unnatural hate:
These shall perform your task.

FIRST FURY
                    Oh, mercy ! mercy !   350
We die with our desire: drive us not back !

MERCURY

Crouch then in silence.
               Awful Sufferer!
To thee unwilling, most unwillingly
I come, by the great Father's will driven down,
To execute a doom of new revenge.   355
Alas! I pity thee, and hate myself
That I can do no more: aye from thy sight
Returning, for a season, Heaven seems Hell,
So thy worn form pursues me night and day,
Smiling reproach. Wise art thou, firm and good,   360
But vainly wouldst stand forth alone in strife
Against the Omnipotent; as yon clear lamps
That measure and divide the weary years
From which there is no refuge, long have taught
And long must teach. Even now thy Torturer arms   365
With the strange might of unimagined pains
The powers who scheme slow agonies in Hell,
And my commission is to lead them here,
Or what more subtle, foul, or savage fiends
People the abyss, and leave them to their task.   370
Be it not so! there is a secret known
To thee, and to none else of living things,
Which may transfer the sceptre of wide Heaven,
The fear of which perplexes the Supreme:
Clothe it in words, and bid it clasp his throne   375
In intercession; bend thy soul in prayer,
And like a suppliant in some gorgeous fane,
Let the will kneel within thy haughty heart:
For benefits and meek submission tame
The fiercest and the mightiest.

PROMETHEUS
             Evil minds   380
Change good to their own nature. I gave all
He has; and in return he chains me here
Years, ages, night and day: whether the Sun
Split my parched skin, or in the moony night
The crystal-wingèd snow cling round my hair: 385
Whilst my belovèd race is trampled down
By his thought-executing ministers.
Such is the tyrant's recompense: 'tis just:
He who is evil can receive no good;
And for a world bestowed, or a friend lost,   390
He can feel hate, fear, shame; not gratitude:
He but requites me for his own misdeed.
Kindness to such is keen reproach, which breaks
With bitter stings the light sleep of Revenge.
Submission, thou dost know I cannot try: 395
For what submission but that fatal word,
The death-seal of mankind's captivity,
Like the Sicilian's hair-suspended sword,
Which trembles o'er his crown, would he accept,
Or could I yield? Which yet I will not yield.   400
Let others flatter Crime, where it sits throned
In brief Omnipotence: secure are they:
For Justice, when triumphant, will weep down
Pity, not punishment, on her own wrongs,
Too much avenged by those who err. I wait,   405
Enduring thus, the retributive hour
Which since we spake is even nearer now.
But hark, the hell-hounds clamour: fear delay:
Behold! Heaven lowers under thy Father's frown.

MERCURY
Oh, that we might be spared; I to inflict 410
And thou to suffer! Once more answer me:
Thou knowest not the period of Jove's power?

PROMETHEUS
I know but this, that it must come.

MERCURY
                        Alas!
Thou canst not count thy years to come of pain?

PROMETHEUS
They last while Jove must reign: nor more, nor less 415
Do I desire or fear.

MERCURY
          Yet pause, and plunge
Into Eternity, where recorded time,
Even all that we imagine, age on age,
Seems but a point, and the reluctant mind
Flags wearily in its unending flight, 420
Till it sink, dizzy, blind, lost, shelterless;
Perchance it has not numbered the slow years
Which thou must spend in torture, unreprieved?

PROMETHEUS
Perchance no thought can count them, yet they pass.

MERCURY
If thou might'st dwell among the Gods the while

Lapped in voluptuous joy? 425

PROMETHEUS
          I would not quit
This bleak ravine, these unrepentant pains.

MERCURY
Alas! I wonder at, yet pity thee.

PROMETHEUS
Pity the self-despising slaves of Heaven,
Not me, within whose mind sits peace serene. 430
As light in the sun, throned: how vain is talk!
Call up the fiends.

IONE
         O, sister, look! White fire
Has cloven to the roots yon huge snow-loaded cedar;
How fearfully God's thunder howls behind!

MERCURY
I must obey his words and thine: alas! 435
Most heavily remorse hangs at my heart!

PANTHEA
See where the child of Heaven, with wingèd feet,
Runs down the slanted sunlight of the dawn.

IONE
Dear sister, close thy plumes over thine eyes
Lest thou behold and die: they come: they come 440

Blackening the birth of day with countless wings,
And hollow underneath, like death.

     FIRST FURY
        Prometheus!

     SECOND FURY
Immortal Titan!

     THIRD FURY
  Champion of Heaven's slaves!

     PROMETHEUS
He whom some dreadful voice invokes is here,
Prometheus, the chained Titan. Horrible forms,   445
What and who are ye? Never yet there came
Phantasms so foul through monster-teeming Hell
From the all-miscreative brain of Jove;
Whilst I behold such execrable shapes,
Methinks I grow like what I contemplate,   450
And laugh and stare in loathsome sympathy. ²

     FIRST FURY
We are the ministers of pain, and fear,
And disappointment, and mistrust, and hate,
And clinging crime; and as lean dogs pursue
Through wood and lake some struck and sobbing fawn,

---

²Cf. Nietzsche: *Wer mit Ungeheurn kämpft, mag zusehn, daß er nicht dabei zum Ungeheur wird.* (*Jenseits von Gut und Böse*) Let him who fights with monsters beware, lest he become a monster thereby. (*Beyond Good and Evil*)

We track all things that weep, and bleed, and live,
When the great King betrays them to our will.

PROMETHEUS

Oh! many fearful natures in one name,
I know ye; and these lakes and echoes know
The darkness and the clangour of your wings. 460
But why more hideous than your loathèd selves
Gather ye up in legions from the deep?

SECOND FURY

We knew not that: Sisters, rejoice, rejoice!

PROMETHEUS

Can aught exult in its deformity?

SECOND FURY

The beauty of delight makes lovers glad, 465
Gazing on one another: so are we.
As from the rose which the pale priestess kneels
To gather for her festal crown of flowers
The aëreal crimson falls, flushing her cheek,
So from our victim's destined agony 470
The shade which is our form invests us round,
Else we are shapeless as our mother Night.

PROMETHEUS

I laugh your power, and his who sent you here,
To lowest scorn. Pour forth the cup of pain.

FIRST FURY
Thou thinkest we will rend thee bone from bone, 475
And nerve from nerve, working like fire within?

PROMETHEUS
Pain is my element, as hate is thine;
Ye rend me now; I care not.

SECOND FURY
                Dost imagine
We will but laugh into thy lidless eyes?

PROMETHEUS
I weigh not what ye do, but what ye suffer, 480
Being evil. Cruel was the power which called
You, or aught else so wretched, into light.

THIRD FURY
Thou think'st we will live through thee, one by one,
Like animal life, and though we can obscure not
The soul which burns within, that we will dwell 485
Beside it, like a vain loud multitude
Vexing the self-content of wisest men:
That we will be dread thought beneath thy brain,
And foul desire round thine astonished heart,
And blood within thy labyrinthine veins 490
Crawling like agony?

PROMETHEUS
              Why, ye are thus now;
Yet am I king over myself, and rule

The torturing and conflicting throngs within,
As Jove rules you when Hell grows mutinous.

CHORUS OF FURIES

From the ends of the earth, from the ends of the earth,
Where the night has its grave and the morning its birth,
    Come, come, come !
Oh, ye who shake hills with the scream of your mirth,
When cities sink howling in ruin; and ye
Who with wingless footsteps trample the sea,   500
And close upon Shipwreck and Famine's track,
Sit chattering with joy on the foodless wreck;
    Come, come, come !
  Leave the bed, low, cold, and red,
  Strewed beneath a nation dead;   505
  Leave the hatred, as in ashes
    Fire is left for future burning:
  It will burst in bloodier flashes
    When ye stir it, soon returning:
  Leave the self-contempt implanted   510
  In young spirits, sense-enchanted,
    Misery's yet unkindled fuel:
  Leave Hell's secrets half unchanted
    To the maniac dreamer; cruel
  More than ye can be with hate   515
    Is he with fear.
    Come, come, come !
We are steaming up from Hell's wide gate
And we burthen the blast of the atmosphere,
But vainly we toil till ye come here.   520

IONE
Sister, I hear the thunder of new wings.

PANTHEA
These solid mountains quiver with the sound
Even as the tremulous air: their shadows make
The space within my plumes more black than night.

FIRST FURY
Your call was as a wingèd car, 525
Driven on whirlwinds fast and far;
It rapped us from red gulfs of war.

SECOND FURY
From wide cities, famine-wasted;

THIRD FURY
Groans half heard, and blood untasted;

FOURTH FURY
Kingly conclaves stern and cold, 530
Where blood with gold is bought and sold;

FIFTH FURY
From the furnace, white and hot,
In which —

A FURY
Speak not: whisper not:
I know all that ye would tell,
But to speak might break the spell 535

Which must bend the Invincible,
    The stern of thought;
He yet defies the deepest power of Hell.

FURY

Tear the veil!

ANOTHER FURY

It is torn.

CHORUS

    The pale stars of the morn
Shine on a misery, dire to be borne.   540
Dost thou faint, mighty Titan? We laugh thee to scorn.
Dost thou boast the clear knowledge thou waken'dst for
    man?
Then was kindled within him a thirst which outran
Those perishing waters; a thirst of fierce fever,
Hope, love, doubt, desire, which consume him for ever.
    One came forth of gentle worth
    Smiling on the sanguine earth;
    His words outlived him, like swift poison
        Withering up truth, peace, and pity.
Look! where round the wide horizon   550
    Many a million-peopled city
Vomits smoke in the bright air.
Mark that outcry of despair!
'Tis his mild and gentle ghost
    Wailing for the faith he kindled: 555
Look again, the flames almost
    To a glow-worm's lamp have dwindled:

The survivors round the embers
   Gather in dread.
      Joy, joy, joy! 560
Past ages crowd on thee, but each one remembers,
And the future is dark, and the present is spread
Like a pillow of thorns for thy slumberless head.

     SEMICHORUS I
  Drops of bloody agony flow
  From his white and quivering brow. 565
  Grant a little respite now:
  See a disenchanted nation
  Springs like day from desolation;
To Truth its state is dedicate,
And Freedom leads it forth, her mate; 570
A legioned band of linked brothers
Whom Love calls children –

     SEMICHORUS II
        'Tis another's:
See how kindred murder kin:
'Tis the vintage-time for death and sin:
Blood, like new wine, bubbles within: 575
  Till Despair smothers
The struggling world, which slaves and tyrants win.

All the FURIES *vanish, except one.*

     IONE
Hark, sister! what a low yet dreadful groan
Quite unsuppressed is tearing up the heart

Of the good Titan, as storms tear the deep,   580
And beasts hear the sea moan in inland caves.
Darest thou observe how the fiends torture him?

PANTHEA

Alas! I looked forth twice, but will no more.

IONE

What didst thou see?

PANTHEA

          A woful sight: a youth
With patient looks nailed to a crucifix.   585

IONE

What next?

PANTHEA

          The heaven around, the earth below
Was peopled with thick shapes of human death,
All horrible, and wrought by human hands,
And some appeared the work of human hearts,
For men were slowly killed by frowns and smiles: 590
And other sights too foul to speak and live
Were wandering by. Let us not tempt worse fear
By looking forth: those groans are grief enough.

FURY

Behold an emblem: those who do endure
Deep wrongs for man, and scorn, and chains, but heap
Thousand-fold torment on themselves and him.

PROMETHEUS
Remit the anguish of that lighted stare;
Close those wan lips; let that thorn-wounded brow
Stream not with blood; it mingles with thy tears !
Fix, fix those tortured orbs in peace and death, 600
So thy sick throes shake not that crucifix,
So those pale fingers play not with thy gore.
O, horrible ! Thy name I will not speak,
It hath become a curse. I see, I see
The wise, the mild, the lofty, and the just, 605
Whom thy slaves hate for being like to thee,
Some hunted by foul lies from their heart's home,
An early-chosen, late-lamented home;
As hooded ounces cling to the driven hind;
Some linked to corpses in unwholesome cells: 610
Some – Hear I not the multitude laugh loud? –
Impaled in lingering fire: and mighty realms
Float by my feet, like sea-uprooted isles,
Whose sons are kneaded down in common blood
By the red light of their own burning homes. 615

FURY
Blood thou canst see, and fire; and canst hear groans;
Worse things unheard, unseen, remain behind.

PROMETHEUS
Worse?

FURY
In each human heart terror survives
The ravin it has gorged: the loftiest fear

All that they would disdain to think were true: 620
Hypocrisy and custom make their minds
The fanes of many a worship, now outworn.
They dare not devise good for man's estate,
And yet they know not that they do not dare.
The good want power, but to weep barren tears. 625
The powerful goodness want: worse need for them.
The wise want love; and those who love want wisdom;
And all best things are thus confused to ill.
Many are strong and rich, and would be just,
But live among their suffering fellow-men 630
As if none felt: they know not what they do.

PROMETHEUS
Thy words are like a cloud of winged snakes;
And yet I pity those they torture not.

FURY
Thou pitiest them? I speak no more !
Vanishes.

PROMETHEUS
       Ah woe !
Ah woe ! Alas ! pain, pain ever, for ever ! 635
I close my tearless eyes, but see more clear
Thy works within my woe-illumèd mind,
Thou subtle tyrant ! Peace is in the grave.
The grave hides all things beautiful and good:
I am a God and cannot find it there, 640
Nor would I seek it: for, though dread revenge,
This is defeat, fierce king, not victory.

The sights with which thou torturest gird my soul
With new endurance, till the hour arrives
When they shall be no types of things which are. 645

PANTHEA
Alas! what sawest thou more?

PROMETHEUS
     There are two woes:
To speak, and to behold; thou spare me one.
Names are there, Nature's sacred watchwords, they
Were borne aloft in bright emblazonry;
The nations thronged around, and cried aloud, 650
As with one voice, Truth, liberty, and love!
Suddenly fierce confusion fell from heaven
Among them: there was strife, deceit, and fear:
Tyrants rushed in, and did divide the spoil.
This was the shadow of the truth I saw. 655

THE EARTH
I felt thy torture, son; with such mixed joy
As pain and virtue give. To cheer thy state
I bid ascend those subtle and fair spirits,
Whose homes are the dim caves of human thought,
And who inhabit, as birds wing the wind, 660
Its world-surrounding aether: they behold
Beyond that twilight realm, as in a glass,
The future: may they speak comfort to thee!

PANTHEA
Look, sister, where a troop of spirits gather,

Like flocks of clouds in spring's delightful weather, 665
Thronging in the blue air!

IONE
        And see! more come,
Like fountain-vapours when the winds are dumb,
That climb up the ravine in scattered lines.
And, hark! is it the music of the pines?
Is it the lake? Is it the waterfall? 670

PANTHEA
'Tis something sadder, sweeter far than all.

CHORUS OF SPIRITS
    From unremembered ages we
    Gentle guides and guardians be
    Of heaven-oppressed mortality;
    And we breathe, and sicken not, 675
    The atmosphere of human thought:
    Be it dim, and dank, and gray,
    Like a storm-extinguished day,
    Travelled o'er by dying gleams;
        Be it bright as all between 680
    Cloudless skies and windless streams,
        Silent, liquid, and serene;
    As the birds within the wind,
        As the fish within the wave,
    As the thoughts of man's own mind 685
        Float through all above the grave;
    We make there our liquid lair,
    Voyaging cloudlike and unpent

Through the boundless element:
Thence we bear the prophecy 690
Which begins and ends in thee!

IONE

More yet come, one by one: the air around them
Looks radiant as the air around a star.

FIRST SPIRIT

On a battle-trumpet's blast
I fled hither, fast, fast, fast, 695
'Mid the darkness upward cast.
From the dust of creeds outworn,
From the tyrant's banner torn,
Gathering 'round me, onward borne,
There was mingled many a cry – 700
Freedom! Hope! Death! Victory!
Till they faded through the sky;
And one sound, above, around,
One sound beneath, around, above,
Was moving; 'twas the soul of Love; 705
'Twas the hope, the prophecy,
Which begins and ends in thee.

SECOND SPIRIT

A rainbow's arch stood on the sea,
Which rocked beneath, immovably;
And the triumphant storm did flee, 710
Like a conqueror, swift and proud,
Between, with many a captive cloud,
A shapeless, dark and rapid crowd,

Each by lightning riven in half:
I heard the thunder hoarsely laugh: 715
Mighty fleets were strewn like chaff
And spread beneath a hell of death
O'er the white waters. I alit
On a great ship lightning-split,
And speeded hither on the sigh 720
Of one who gave an enemy
His plank, then plunged aside to die.

THIRD SPIRIT

I sate beside a sage's bed,
And the lamp was burning red
Near the book where he had fed, 725
When a Dream with plumes of flame,
To his pillow hovering came,
And I knew it was the same
Which had kindled long ago
Pity, eloquence, and woe; 730
And the world awhile below
Wore the shade, its lustre made.
It has borne me here as fleet
As Desire's lightning feet:
I must ride it back ere morrow, 735
Or the sage will wake in sorrow.

FOURTH SPIRIT

On a poet's lips I slept
Dreaming like a love-adept
In the sound his breathing kept;
Nor seeks nor finds he mortal blisses, 740

But feeds on the aëreal kisses
Of shapes that haunt thought's wildernesses.
He will watch from dawn to gloom
The lake-reflected sun illume
The yellow bees in the ivy-bloom,   745
Nor heed nor see, what things they be;
But from these create he can
Forms more real than living man,
Nurslings of immortality !
One of these awakened me,   750
And I sped to succour thee.

IONE
Behold'st thou not two shapes from the east and west
Come, as two doves to one beloved nest,
Twin nurslings of the all-sustaining air
On swift still wings glide down the atmosphere?   755
And, hark ! their sweet sad voices ! 'tis despair
Mingled with love and then dissolved in sound.

PANTHEA
Canst thou speak, sister? all my words are drowned.

IONE
Their beauty gives me voice. See how they float
On their sustaining wings of skiey grain,   760
Orange and azure deepening into gold:
Their soft smiles light the air like a star's fire.

CHORUS OF SPIRITS
Hast thou beheld the form of Love?

FIFTH SPIRIT
  As over wide dominions
 I sped, like some swift cloud that wings the wide air's wildernesses,
That planet-crested shape swept by on lightning-braided pinions,   765
 Scattering the liquid joy of life from his ambrosial tresses:
His footsteps paved the world with light; but as I passed 'twas fading,
 And hollow Ruin yawned behind: great sages bound in madness,
And headless patriots, and pale youths who perished, unupbraiding,
 Gleamed in the night. I wandered o'er, till thou, O King of sadness,   770
Turned by thy smile the worst I saw to recollected gladness.

SIXTH SPIRIT
Ah, sister! Desolation is a delicate thing:
 It walks not on the earth, it floats not on the air,
But treads with lulling footstep, and fans with silent wing
 The tender hopes which in their hearts the best and gentlest bear;   775
Who, soothed to false repose by the fanning plumes above
 And the music-stirring motion of its soft and busy feet,
Dream visions of aëreal joy, and call the monster, Love,
 And wake, and find the shadow Pain, as he whom now we greet.

CHORUS
 Though Ruin now Love's shadow be,   780

Following him, destroyingly,
    On Death's white and wingèd steed,
Which the fleetest cannot flee,
    Trampling down both flower and weed,
Man and beast, and foul and fair,   785
Like a tempest through the air;
Thou shalt quell this horseman grim,
Woundless though in heart or limb.

PROMETHEUS
Spirits! how know ye this shall be?

CHORUS
    In the atmosphere we breathe,   790
As buds grow red when the snow-storms flee,
    From Spring gathering up beneath,
Whose mild winds shake the elder-brake,
And the wandering herdsmen know
That the whitethorn soon will blow: 795
    Wisdom, Justice, Love, and Peace,
When they struggle to increase,
    Are to us as soft winds be
    To shepherd boys, the prophecy
    Which begins and ends in thee.   800

IONE
Where are the Spirits fled?

PANTHEA
Only a sense

Remains of them, like the omnipotence
Of music, when the inspired voice and lute
Languish, ere yet the responses are mute,
Which through the deep and labyrinthine soul, 805
Like echoes through long caverns, wind and roll.

PROMETHEUS

How fair these airborn shapes! and yet I feel
Most vain all hope but love; and thou art far,
Asia! who, when my being overflowed,
Wert like a golden chalice to bright wine 810
Which else had sunk into the thirsty dust.
All things are still: alas! how heavily
This quiet morning weighs upon my heart;
Though I should dream I could even sleep with grief
If slumber were denied not. I would fain 815
Be what it is my destiny to be,
The saviour and the strength of suffering man,
Or sink into the original gulf of things:
There is no agony, and no solace left;
Earth can console, Heaven can torment no more. 820

PANTHEA

Hast thou forgotten one who watches thee
The cold dark night, and never sleeps but when
The shadow of thy spirit falls on her?

PROMETHEUS

I said all hope was vain but love: thou lovest.

PANTHEA
Deeply in truth; but the eastern star looks white, 825
And Asia waits in that far Indian vale,
The scene of her sad exile; rugged once
And desolate and frozen, like this ravine;
But now invested with fair flowers and herbs,
And haunted by sweet airs and sounds, which flow 830
Among the woods and waters, from the aether
Of her transforming presence, which would fade
If it were mingled not with thine. Farewell!

END OF THE FIRST ACT

ACT II

SCENE I
Morning. A lovely Vale in the Indian Caucasus.
ASIA alone.

ASIA
From all the blasts of heaven thou hast descended:
Yes, like a spirit, like a thought, which makes
Unwonted tears throng to the horny eyes,
And beatings haunt the desolated heart,
Which should have learnt repose: thou hast descended 5
Cradled in tempests; thou dost wake, O Spring!
O child of many winds! As suddenly
Thou comest as the memory of a dream,
Which now is sad because it hath been sweet;
Like genius, or like joy which riseth up 10

As from the earth, clothing with golden clouds
The desert of our life.
This is the season, this the day, the hour;
At sunrise thou shouldst come, sweet sister mine,
Too long desired, too long delaying, come ! 15
How like death-worms the wingless moments crawl !
The point of one white star is quivering still
Deep in the orange light of widening morn
Beyond the purple mountains: through a chasm
Of wind-divided mist the darker lake 20
Reflects it: now it wanes: it gleams again
As the waves fade, and as the burning threads
Of woven cloud unravel in pale air:
'Tis lost ! and through yon peaks of cloud-like snow
The roseate sunlight quivers: hear I not 25
The Æolian music of her sea-green plumes
Winnowing the crimson dawn?

PANTHEA *enters*.
I feel, I see
Those eyes which burn through smiles that fade in tears,
Like stars half quenched in mists of silver dew.
Beloved and most beautiful, who wearest 30
The shadow of that soul by which I live,
How late thou art ! the sphered sun had climbed
The sea; my heart was sick with hope, before
The printless air felt thy belated plumes.

PANTHEA
Pardon, great Sister ! but my wings were faint 35
With the delight of a remembered dream,

        As are the noontide plumes of summer winds
        Satiate with sweet flowers. I was wont to sleep
        Peacefully, and awake refreshed and calm
        Before the sacred Titan's fall, and thy   40
        Unhappy love, had made, through use and pity,
        Both love and woe familiar to my heart
        As they had grown to thine: erewhile I slept
        Under the glaucous caverns of old Ocean
        Within dim bowers of green and purple moss,   45
        Our young Ione's soft and milky arms
        Locked then, as now, behind my dark, moist hair,
        While my shut eyes and cheek were pressed within
        The folded depth of her life-breathing bosom:
        But not as now, since I am made the wind   50
        Which fails beneath the music that I bear
        Of thy most wordless converse; since dissolved
        Into the sense with which love talks, my rest
        Was troubled and yet sweet; my waking hours
        Too full of care and pain.

                        ASIA
                                Lift up thine eyes,   55
        And let me read thy dream.

                        PANTHEA
                                As I have said
        With our sea-sister at his feet I slept.
        The mountain mists, condensing at our voice
        Under the moon, had spread their snowy flakes,
        From the keen ice shielding our linkèd sleep.   60
        Then two dreams came. One, I remember not.

But in the other his pale wound-worn limbs
Fell from Prometheus, and the azure night
Grew radiant with the glory of that form
Which lives unchanged within, and his voice fell   65
Like music which makes giddy the dim brain,
Faint with intoxication of keen joy:
'Sister of her whose footsteps pave the world
With loveliness – more fair than aught but her,
Whose shadow thou art – lift thine eyes on me.'   70
I lifted them: the overpowering light
Of that immortal shape was shadowed o'er
By love; which, from his soft and flowing limbs,
And passion-parted lips, and keen, faint eyes,
Steamed forth like vaporous fire; an atmosphere   75
Which wrapped me in its all-dissolving power,
As the warm aether of the morning sun
Wraps ere it drinks some cloud of wandering dew.
I saw not, heard not, moved not, only felt
His presence flow and mingle through my blood   80
Till it became his life, and his grew mine,
And I was thus absorbed, until it passed,
And like the vapours when the sun sinks down,
Gathering again in drops upon the pines,
And tremulous as they, in the deep night   85
My being was condensed; and as the rays
Of thought were slowly gathered, I could hear
His voice, whose accents lingered ere they died
Like footsteps of weak melody: thy name
Among the many sounds alone I heard   90
Of what might be articulate; though still
I listened through the night when sound was none.

Ione wakened then, and said to me:
'Canst thou divine what troubles me to-night?
I always knew, what I desired before, 95
Nor ever found delight to wish in vain.
But now I cannot tell thee what I seek;
I know not; something sweet, since it is sweet
Even to desire; it is thy sport, false sister;
Thou hast discovered some enchantment old, 100
Whose spells have stolen my spirit as I slept
And mingled it with thine: for when just now
We kissed, I felt within thy parted lips
The sweet air that sustained me, and the warmth
Of the life-blood, for loss of which I faint, 105
Quivered between our intertwining arms.'
I answered not, for the Eastern star grew pale,
But fled to thee.

ASIA

          Thou speakest, but thy words
Are as the air: I feel them not: Oh, lift
Thine eyes, that I may read his written soul! 110

PANTHEA

I lift them though they droop beneath the load
Of that they would express: what canst thou see
But thine own fairest shadow imaged there?

ASIA

Thine eyes are like the deep, blue, boundless heaven
Contracted to two circles underneath 115
Their long, fine lashes; dark, far, measureless,

Orb within orb, and line through line inwoven.

PANTHEA
Why lookest thou as if a spirit passed?

ASIA
There is a change: beyond their inmost depth
I see a shade, a shape: 'tis He, arrayed   120
In the soft light of his own smiles, which spread
Like radiance from the cloud-surrounded moon.
Prometheus, it is thine ! depart not yet !
Say not those smiles that we shall meet again
Within that bright pavilion which their beams   125
Shall build o'er the waste world? The dream is told.
What shape is that between us? Its rude hair
Roughens the wind that lifts it, its regard
Is wild and quick, yet 'tis a thing of air,
For through its gray robe gleams the golden dew   130
Whose stars the noon has quenched not.

DREAM
                     Follow ! Follow !

PANTHEA
It is mine other dream.

ASIA
It disappears.

PANTHEA
It passes now into my mind. Methought

As we sate here, the flower-infolding buds
Burst on yon lightning-blasted almond tree, 135
When swift from the white Scythian wilderness
A wind swept forth wrinkling the Earth with frost:
I looked, and all the blossoms were blown down;
But on each leaf was stamped, as the blue bells
Of Hyacinth tell Apollo's written grief, 140
O, FOLLOW, FOLLOW !

ASIA
              As you speak, your words
Fill, pause by pause, my own forgotten sleep
With shapes. Methought among these lawns together
We wandered, underneath the young gray dawn,
And multitudes of dense white fleecy clouds 145
Were wandering in thick flocks along the mountains
Shepherded by the slow, unwilling wind;
And the white dew on the new-bladed grass,
Just piercing the dark earth, hung silently;
And there was more which I remember not: 150
But on the shadows of the morning clouds,
Athwart the purple mountain slope, was written
FOLLOW, O, FOLLOW ! as they vanished by;
And on each herb, from which Heaven's dew had fallen,
The like was stamped, as with a withering fire; 155
A wind arose among the pines; it shook
The clinging music from their boughs, and then
Low, sweet, faint sounds, like the farewell of ghosts,
Were heard: O, FOLLOW, FOLLOW, FOLLOW ME !
And then I said, 'Panthea, look on me.' 160
But in the depth of those beloved eyes

Still I saw, FOLLOW, FOLLOW !

          ECHO
        Follow, follow !

        PANTHEA
The crags, this clear spring morning, mock our voices
As they were spirit-tongued.

          ASIA
        It is some being
Around the crags. What fine clear sounds ! O, list !   165

      ECHOES (unseen)
     Echoes we: listen !
      We cannot stay:
    As dew-stars glisten
      Then fade away –
        Child of Ocean !   170

          ASIA
Hark ! Spirits speak. The liquid responses
Of their aëreal tongues yet sound.

        PANTHEA
          I hear.

        ECHOES
   Oh, follow, follow,
     As our voice recedeth
   Through the caverns hollow,   175

Where the forest spreadeth;
   (*More distant*)
Oh, follow, follow !
Through the caverns hollow,
As the song floats thou pursue,
Where the wild bee never flew, 180
Through the noontide darkness deep,
By the odour-breathing sleep
Of faint night-flowers, and the waves
At the fountain-lighted caves,
While our music, wild and sweet, 185
Mocks thy gently falling feet,
   Child of Ocean !

ASIA
Shall we pursue the sound? It grows more faint
And distant.

PANTHEA
List ! the strain floats nearer now.

ECHOES
In the world unknown 190
   Sleeps a voice unspoken;
By thy step alone
   Can its rest be broken;
   Child of Ocean !

ASIA
How the notes sink upon the ebbing wind ! 195

ECHOES

Oh, follow, follow!
Through the caverns hollow,
As the song floats thou pursue,
By the woodland noontide dew;
By the forests, lakes, and fountains, 200
Through the many-folded mountains;
To the rents, and gulfs, and chasms,
Where the Earth reposed from spasms,
On the day when He and thou
Parted, to commingle now; 205
Child of Ocean!

ASIA

Come, sweet Panthea, link thy hand in mine,
And follow, ere the voices fade away.

SCENE II

A Forest, intermingled with Rocks and Caverns.
Asia *and* Panthea *pass into it.*
Two young Fauns are sitting on a Rock listening.

SEMICHORUS I OF SPIRITS

The path through which that lovely twain
Have passed, by cedar, pine, and yew,
And each dark tree that ever grew,
Is curtained out from Heaven's wide blue;
Nor sun, nor moon, nor wind, nor rain, 5
Can pierce its interwoven bowers,
Nor aught, save where some cloud of dew,
Drifted along the earth-creeping breeze,

Between the trunks of the hoar trees,
    Hangs each a pearl in the pale flowers 10
  Of the green laurel, blown anew,
And bends, and then fades silently,
One frail and fair anemone:
Or when some star of many a one
That climbs and wanders through steep night, 15
Has found the cleft through which alone
Beams fall from high those depths upon
Ere it is borne away, away,
By the swift Heavens that cannot stay,
It scatters drops of golden light, 20
Like lines of rain that ne'er unite:
And the gloom divine is all around,
And underneath is the mossy ground.

SEMICHORUS II
There the voluptuous nightingales,
  Are awake through all the broad noonday. 25
When one with bliss or sadness fails,
    And through the windless ivy-boughs,
  Sick with sweet love, droops dying away
On its mate's music-panting bosom;
Another from the swinging blossom, 30
    Watching to catch the languid close
  Of the last strain, then lifts on high
  The wings of the weak melody,
'Till some new strain of feeling bear
  The song, and all the woods are mute; 35
When there is heard through the dim air
The rush of wings, and rising there

       Like many a lake-surrounded flute,
Sounds overflow the listener's brain
So sweet, that joy is almost pain. 40

SEMICHORUS I
There those enchanted eddies play
    Of echoes, music-tongued, which draw,
    By Demogorgon's mighty law,
    With melting rapture, or sweet awe,
All spirits on that secret way; 45
    As inland boats are driven to Ocean
Down streams made strong with mountain-thaw:
      And first there comes a gentle sound
      To those in talk or slumber bound,
    And wakes the destined soft emotion, – 50
Attracts, impels them; those who saw
    Say from the breathing earth behind
    There steams a plume-uplifting wind
Which drives them on their path, while they
    Believe their own swift wings and feet 55
The sweet desires within obey:
And so they float upon their way,
Until, still sweet, but loud and strong,
The storm of sound is driven along,
    Sucked up and hurrying: as they fleet 60
    Behind, its gathering billows meet
And to the fatal mountain bear
Like clouds amid the yielding air.

FIRST FAUN
Canst thou imagine where those spirits live

Which make such delicate music in the woods? 65
We haunt within the least frequented caves
And closest coverts, and we know these wilds,
Yet never meet them, though we hear them oft:
Where may they hide themselves?

SECOND FAUN
'Tis hard to tell;
I have heard those more skilled in spirits say, 70
The bubbles, which the enchantment of the sun
Sucks from the pale faint water-flowers that pave
The oozy bottom of clear lakes and pools,
Are the pavilions where such dwell and float
Under the green and golden atmosphere 75
Which noontide kindles through the woven leaves;
And when these burst, and the thin fiery air,
The which they breathed within those lucent domes,
Ascends to flow like meteors through the night,
They ride on them, and rein their headlong speed, 80
And bow their burning crests, and glide in fire
Under the waters of the earth again.

FIRST FAUN
If such live thus, have others other lives,
Under pink blossoms or within the bells
Of meadow flowers, or folded violets deep, 85
Or on their dying odours, when they die,
Or in the sunlight of the spherèd dew?

SECOND FAUN
Ay, many more which we may well divine.

But should we stay to speak, noontide would come,
And thwart Silenus find his goats undrawn,　　　　　90
And grudge to sing those wise and lovely songs
Of Fate, and Chance, and God, and Chaos old,
And Love, and the chained Titan's woful doom,
And how he shall be loosed, and make the earth
One brotherhood: delightful strains which cheer　　　95
Our solitary twilights, and which charm
To silence the unenvying nightingales.

SCENE III

A Pinnacle of Rock among Mountains. ASIA *and* PANTHEA.

PANTHEA

Hither the sound has borne us – to the realm
Of Demogorgon, and the mighty portal,
Like a volcano's meteor-breathing chasm,
Whence the oracular vapour is hurled up
Which lonely men drink wandering in their youth,　　　5
And call truth, virtue, love, genius, or joy,
That maddening wine of life, whose dregs they drain
To deep intoxication; and uplift,
Like Mænads who cry loud, Evoe! Evoe!
The voice which is contagion to the world.　　　10

ASIA

Fit throne for such a Power! Magnificent!
How glorious art thou, Earth! And if thou be
The shadow of some spirit lovelier still,
Though evil stain its work, and it should be
Like its creation, weak yet beautiful,　　　15

I could fall down and worship that and thee.
Even now my heart adoreth: Wonderful !
Look, sister, ere the vapour dim thy brain:
Beneath is a wide plain of billowy mist,
As a lake, paving in the morning sky,   20
With azure waves which burst in silver light,
Some Indian vale. Behold it, rolling on
Under the curdling winds, and islanding
The peak whereon we stand, midway, around,
Encinctured by the dark and blooming forests,   25
Dim twilight-lawns, and stream-illumined caves,
And wind-enchanted shapes of wandering mist;
And far on high the keen sky-cleaving mountains
From icy spires of sun-like radiance fling
The dawn, as lifted Ocean's dazzling spray,   30
From some Atlantic islet scattered up,
Spangles the wind with lamp-like water-drops.
The vale is girdled with their walls, a howl
Of cataracts from their thaw-cloven ravines,
Satiates the listening wind, continuous, vast,   35
Awful as silence. Hark ! the rushing snow !
The sun-awakened avalanche ! whose mass,
Thrice sifted by the storm, had gathered there
Flake after flake, in heaven-defying minds
As thought by thought is piled, till some great truth   40
Is loosened, and the nations echo round,
Shaken to their roots, as do the mountains now.

PANTHEA
Look how the gusty sea of mist is breaking
In crimson foam, even at our feet ! it rises

As Ocean at the enchantment of the moon 45
Round foodless men wrecked on some oozy isle.

ASIA

The fragments of the cloud are scattered up;
The wind that lifts them disentwines my hair;
Its billows now sweep o'er mine eyes; my brain
Grows dizzy; see'st thou shapes within the mist? 50

PANTHEA

A countenance with beckoning smiles: there burns
An azure fire within its golden locks !
Another and another: hark ! they speak !

SONG OF SPIRITS

 To the deep, to the deep,
   Down, down ! 55
 Through the shade of sleep,
 Through the cloudy strife
 Of Death and of Life;
 Through the veil and the bar
 Of things which seem and are 60
Even to the steps of the remotest throne,
   Down, down !

 While the sound whirls around,
   Down, down !
 As the fawn draws the hound, 65
 As the lightning the vapour,
 As a weak moth the taper;
 Death, despair; love, sorrow;

Time both; to-day, to-morrow;
As steel obeys the spirit of the stone, 70
  Down, down!

Through the gray, void abysm,
  Down, down!
Where the air is no prism,
And the moon and stars are not, 75
And the cavern-crags wear not
The radiance of Heaven,
Nor the gloom to Earth given,
Where there is One pervading, One alone,
  Down, down! 80

In the depth of the deep,
  Down, down!
Like veiled lightning asleep,
Like the spark nursed in embers,
The last look Love remembers, 85
Like a diamond, which shines
On the dark wealth of mines,
A spell is treasured but for thee alone.
  Down, down!

We have bound thee, we guide thee; 90
  Down, down!
With the bright form beside thee;
Resist not the weakness,
Such strength is in meekness
That the Eternal, the Immortal, 95
Must unloose through life's portal

> The snake-like Doom coiled underneath his throne
> By that alone.

SCENE IV

The Cave of DEMOGORGON. ASIA *and* PANTHEA.

PANTHEA

What veilèd form sits on that ebon throne?

ASIA

The veil has fallen.

PANTHEA

     I see a mighty darkness
Filling the seat of power, and rays of gloom
Dart round, as light from the meridian sun.
– Ungazed upon and shapeless; neither limb,   5
Nor form, nor outline; yet we feel it is
A living Spirit.

DEMOGORGON

Ask what thou wouldst know.

ASIA

What canst thou tell?

DEMOGORGON

All things thou dar'st demand.

ASIA

Who made the living world?

DEMOGORGON
God.

ASIA
Who made all
That it contains? thought, passion, reason, will,　　10
Imagination?

DEMOGORGON
God: Almighty God.

ASIA
Who made that sense which, when the winds of Spring
In rarest visitation, or the voice
Of one belovèd heard in youth alone,
Fills the faint eyes with falling tears which dim　　15
The radiant looks of unbewailing flowers,
And leaves this peopled earth a solitude
When it returns no more?

DEMOGORGON
Merciful God.

ASIA
And who made terror, madness, crime, remorse,
Which from the links of the great chain of things,　　20
To every thought within the mind of man
Sway and drag heavily, and each one reels
Under the load towards the pit of death;
Abandoned hope, and love that turns to hate;
And self-contempt, bitterer to drink than blood;　　25

Pain, whose unheeded and familiar speech
Is howling, and keen shrieks, day after day;
And Hell, or the sharp fear of Hell?

           DEMOGORGON
                         He reigns.

           ASIA
Utter his name: a world pining in pain
Asks but his name: curses shall drag him down.   30

           DEMOGORGON
He reigns.

           ASIA
    I feel, I know it: who?

           DEMOGORGON
                         He reigns.

           ASIA
Who reigns? There was the Heaven and Earth at first,
And Light and Love; then Saturn, from whose throne
Time fell, an envious shadow: such the state
Of the earth's primal spirits beneath his sway,   35
As the calm joy of flowers and living leaves
Before the wind or sun has withered them
And semivital worms; but he refused
The birthright of their being, knowledge, power,
The skill which wields the elements, the thought   40
Which pierces this dim universe like light,

Self-empire, and the majesty of love;
For thirst of which they fainted. Then Prometheus
Gave wisdom, which is strength, to Jupiter,
And with this law alone, 'Let man be free,' 45
Clothed him with the dominion of wide Heaven.
To know nor faith, nor love, nor law; to be
Omnipotent but friendless is to reign;
And Jove now reigned; for on the race of man
First famine, and then toil, and then disease, 50
Strife, wounds, and ghastly death unseen before,
Fell; and the unseasonable seasons drove
With alternating shafts of frost and fire,
Their shelterless, pale tribes to mountain caves:
And in their desert hearts fierce wants he sent, 55
And mad disquietudes, and shadows idle
Of unreal good, which levied mutual war,
So ruining the lair wherein they raged.
Prometheus saw, and waked the legioned hopes
Which sleep within folded Elysian flowers, 60
Nepenthe, Moly, Amaranth, fadeless blooms,
That they might hide with thin and rainbow wings
The shape of Death; and Love he sent to bind
The disunited tendrils of that vine
Which bears the wine of life, the human heart; 65
And he tamed fire which, like some beast of prey,
Most terrible, but lovely, played beneath
The frown of man; and tortured to his will
Iron and gold, the slaves and signs of power,
And gems and poisons, and all subtlest forms 70
Hidden beneath the mountains and the waves.
He gave man speech, and speech created thought,

Which is the measure of the universe;
And Science struck the thrones of earth and heaven,
Which shook, but fell not; and the harmonious mind   75
Poured itself forth in all-prophetic song;
And music lifted up the listening spirit
Until it walked, exempt from mortal care,
Godlike, o'er the clear billows of sweet sound;
And human hands first mimicked and then mocked,   80
With moulded limbs more lovely than its own,
The human form, till marble grew divine;
And mothers, gazing, drank the love men see
Reflected in their race, behold, and perish.
He told the hidden power of herbs and springs,   85
And Disease drank and slept. Death grew like sleep.
He taught the implicated orbits woven
Of the wide-wandering stars; and how the sun
Changes his lair, and by what secret spell
The pale moon is transformed, when her broad eye   90
Gazes not on the interlunar sea:
He taught to rule, as life directs the limbs,
The tempest-wingèd chariots of the Ocean,
And the Celt knew the Indian. Cities then
Were built, and through their snow-like columns flowed
The warm winds, and the azure aether shone,
And the blue sea and shadowy hills were seen.
Such, the alleviations of his state,
Prometheus gave to man, for which he hangs
Withering in destined pain: but who rains down   100
Evil, the immedicable plague, which, while
Man looks on his creation like a God
And sees that it is glorious, drives him on,

The wreck of his own will, the scorn of earth,
The outcast, the abandoned, the alone? 105
Not Jove: while yet his frown shook Heaven ay, when
His adversary from adamantine chains
Cursed him, he trembled like a slave. Declare
Who is his master? Is he too a slave?

DEMOGORGON:
All spirits are enslaved which serve things evil: 110
Thou knowest if Jupiter be such or no.

ASIA
Whom calledst thou God?

DEMOGORGON
     I spoke but as ye speak,
For Jove is the supreme of living things.

ASIA
Who is the master of the slave?

DEMOGORGON
     If the abysm
Could vomit forth its secrets. . . . But a voice 115
Is wanting, the deep truth is imageless;
For what would it avail to bid thee gaze
On the revolving world? What to bid speak
Fate, Time, Occasion, Chance and Change? To these
All things are subject but eternal Love. 120

ASIA

So much I asked before, and my heart gave
The response thou hast given; and of such truths
Each to itself must be the oracle.
One more demand; and do thou answer me
As my own soul would answer, did it know   125
That which I ask. Prometheus shall arise
Henceforth the sun of this rejoicing world:
When shall the destined hour arrive?

DEMOGORGON
                      Behold!

ASIA

The rocks are cloven, and through the purple night
I see cars drawn by rainbow-wingèd steeds   130
Which trample the dim winds: in each there stands
A wild-eyed charioteer urging their flight.
Some look behind, as fiends pursued them there,
And yet I see no shapes but the keen stars:
Others, with burning eyes, lean forth, and drink   135
With eager lips the wind of their own speed,
As if the thing they loved fled on before,
And now, even now, they clasped it. Their bright locks
Stream like a comet's flashing hair; they all
Sweep onward.

DEMOGORGON
          These are the immortal Hours,   140
Of whom thou didst demand. One waits for thee.

ASIA

A Spirit with a dreadful countenance
Checks its dark chariot by the craggy gulf.
Unlike thy brethren, ghastly charioteer,
Who art thou? Whither wouldst thou bear me? Speak!

SPIRIT

I am the shadow of a destiny
More dread than is my aspect: ere yon planet
Has set, the darkness which ascends with me
Shall wrap in lasting night heaven's kingless throne.

ASIA

What meanest thou?

PANTHEA

              That terrible shadow floats   150
Up from its throne, as may the lurid smoke
Of earthquake-ruined cities o'er the sea.
Lo! it ascends the car; the coursers fly
Terrified: watch its path among the stars
Blackening the night!

ASIA

              Thus I am answered: strange!   155

PANTHEA

See, near the verge, another chariot stays;
An ivory shell inlaid with crimson fire,
Which comes and goes within its sculptured rim
Of delicate strange tracery; the young spirit

That guides it has the dove-like eyes of hope; 160
How its soft smiles attract the soul! as light
Lures wingèd insects through the lampless air.

SPIRIT

My coursers are fed with the lightning,
    They drink of the whirlwind's stream,
And when the red morning is bright'ning 165
    They bathe in the fresh sunbeam;
    They have strength for their swiftness I deem;
Then ascend with me, daughter of Ocean.

I desire: and their speed makes night kindle;
    I fear: they outstrip the Typhoon; 170
Ere the cloud piled on Atlas can dwindle
    We encircle the earth and the moon:
    We shall rest from long labours at noon:
Then ascend with me, daughter of Ocean.

SCENE V

The Car pauses within a Cloud on the top of a snowy Mountain.
    ASIA, PANTHEA, *and the* SPIRIT OF THE HOUR.

SPIRIT

On the brink of the night and the morning
    My coursers are wont to respire;
But the Earth has just whispered a warning
    That their flight must be swifter than fire:
    They shall drink the hot speed of desire! 5

ASIA
Thou breathest on their nostrils, but my breath
Would give them swifter speed.

SPIRIT
                          Alas! it could not.

PANTHEA
Oh Spirit! pause, and tell whence is the light
Which fills this cloud? the sun is yet unrisen.

SPIRIT
The sun will rise not until noon. Apollo   10
Is held in heaven by wonder; and the light
Which fills this vapour, as the aëreal hue
Of fountain-gazing roses fills the water,
Flows from thy mighty sister.

PANTHEA
                        Yes, I feel –

ASIA
What is it with thee, sister? Thou art pale.   15

PANTHEA
How thou art changed! I dare not look on thee;
I feel but see thee not. I scarce endure
The radiance of thy beauty. Some good change
Is working in the elements, which suffer
Thy presence thus unveiled. The Nereids tell   20
That on the day when the clear hyaline

Was cloven at thine uprise, and thou didst stand
Within a veinèd shell, which floated on
Over the calm floor of the crystal sea,
Among the Ægean isles, and by the shores   25
Which bear thy name; love, like the atmosphere
Of the sun's fire filling the living world,
Burst from thee, and illumined earth and heaven
And the deep ocean and the sunless caves
And all that dwells within them; till grief cast   30
Eclipse upon the soul from which it came:
Such art thou now; nor is it I alone,
Thy sister, thy companion, thine own chosen one,
But the whole world which seeks thy sympathy.
Hearest thou not sounds i' the air which speak the love
Of all articulate beings? Feelest thou not
The inanimate winds enamoured of thee? List!

(Music)

ASIA

Thy words are sweeter than aught else but his
Whose echoes they are; yet all love is sweet,
Given or returned. Common as light is love,   40
And its familiar voice wearies not ever.
Like the wide heaven, the all-sustaining air,
It makes the reptile equal to the God:
They who inspire it most are fortunate,
As I am now; but those who feel it most   45
Are happier still, after long sufferings,
As I shall soon become.

PANTHEA
　　List ! Spirits speak.

VOICE IN THE AIR, *singing*
Life of Life ! thy lips enkindle
　　With their love the breath between them;
And thy smiles before they dwindle　　　　　　　　50
　　Make the cold air fire; then screen them
In those looks, where whoso gazes
Faints, entangled in their mazes.

Child of Light ! thy limbs are burning
　　Through the vest which seems to hide them;　　55
As the radiant lines of morning
　　Through the clouds ere they divide them;
And this atmosphere divinest
Shrouds thee wheresoe'er thou shinest.

Fair are others; none beholds thee,　　　　　　　　60
　　But thy voice sounds low and tender
Like the fairest, for it folds thee
　　From the sight, that liquid splendour,
And all feel, yet see thee never,
As I feel now, lost for ever !　　　　　　　　　　　65

Lamp of Earth ! where'er thou movest
　　Its dim shapes are clad with brightness,
And the souls of whom thou lovest
　　Walk upon the winds with lightness,
Till they fail, as I am failing,　　　　　　　　　　70
Dizzy, lost, yet unbewailing !

ASIA

   My soul is an enchanted boat,
    Which, like a sleeping swan, doth float
Upon the silver waves of thy sweet singing;
    And thine doth like an angel sit   75
    Beside a helm conducting it,
Whilst all the winds with melody are ringing.
    It seems to float ever, for ever,
    Upon that many-winding river,
    Between mountains, woods, abysses,   80
    A paradise of wildernesses !
Till, like one in slumber bound,
Borne to the ocean, I float down, around,
Into a sea profound, of ever-spreading sound:

    Meanwhile thy spirit lifts its pinions   85
    In music's most serene dominions;
Catching the winds that fan that happy heaven.
    And we sail on, away, afar,
    Without a course, without a star,
But, by the instinct of sweet music driven;   90
    Till through Elysian garden islets
    By thee most beautiful of pilots,
    Where never mortal pinnace glided,
    The boat of my desire is guided:
Realms where the air we breathe is love,   95
Which in the winds on the waves doth move,
Harmonizing this earth with what we feel above.

    We have passed Age's icy caves,
    And Manhood's dark and tossing waves,

And Youth's smooth ocean, smiling to betray: 100
    Beyond the glassy gulfs we flee
    Of shadow-peopled Infancy,
Through Death and Birth, to a diviner day;
    A paradise of vaulted bowers,
    Lit by downward-gazing flowers, 105
    And watery paths that wind between
    Wildernesses calm and green,
Peopled by shapes too bright to see,
And rest, having beheld; somewhat like thee;
Which walk upon the sea, and chant melodiously! 110

END OF THE SECOND ACT

ACT III

SCENE I
Heaven. JUPITER *on his Throne;*
THETIS *and the other Deities assembled.*

JUPITER
Ye congregated powers of heaven, who share
The glory and the strength of him ye serve,
Rejoice! henceforth I am omnipotent.
All else had been subdued to me; alone
The soul of man, like unextinguished fire, 5
Yet burns towards heaven with fierce reproach, and doubt,
And lamentation, and reluctant prayer,
Hurling up insurrection, which might make

Our antique empire insecure, though built
On eldest faith, and hell's coeval, fear; 10
And though my curses through the pendulous air,
Like snow on herbless peaks, fall flake by flake,
And cling to it; though under my wrath's night
It climbs the crags of life, step after step,
Which wound it, as ice wounds unsandalled feet, 15
It yet remains supreme o'er misery,
Aspiring, unrepressed, yet soon to fall:
Even now have I begotten a strange wonder,
That fatal child, the terror of the earth,
Who waits but till the destined hour arrive, 20
Bearing from Demogorgon's vacant throne
The dreadful might of ever-living limbs
Which clothed that awful spirit unbeheld,
To redescend, and trample out the spark.
Pour forth heaven's wine, Idæan Ganymede, 25
And let it fill the Dædal cups like fire,
And from the flower-inwoven soil divine
Ye all-triumphant harmonies arise,
As dew from earth under the twilight stars:
Drink! be the nectar circling through your veins 30
The soul of joy, ye ever-living Gods,
Till exultation burst in one wide voice
Like music from Elysian winds.
                                And thou
Ascend beside me, veilèd in the light
Of the desire which makes thee one with me, 35
Thetis, bright image of eternity!
When thou didst cry, 'Insufferable might!
God! Spare me! I sustain not the quick flames,

The penetrating presence; all my being,
Like him whom the Numidian seps did thaw   40
Into a dew with poison, is dissolved,
Sinking through its foundations:' even then
Two mighty spirits, mingling, made a third
Mightier than either, which, unbodied now,
Between us floats, felt, although unbeheld,   45
Waiting the incarnation, which ascends,
(Hear ye the thunder of the fiery wheels
Griding the winds?) from Demogorgon's throne.
Victory! victory! Feel'st thou not, O world,
The earthquake of his chariot thundering up   50
Olympus?

The Car of the HOUR *arrives.* DEMOGORGON *descends,
and moves towards the Throne of* JUPITER.

Awful shape, what art thou? Speak!

DEMOGORGON
Eternity. Demand no direr name.
Descend, and follow me down the abyss.
I am thy child, as thou wert Saturn's child;
Mightier than thee: and we must dwell together   55
Henceforth in darkness. Lift thy lightnings not.
The tyranny of heaven none may retain,
Or reassume, or hold, succeeding thee:
Yet if thou wilt, as 'tis the destiny
Of trodden worms to writhe till they are dead,   60
Put forth thy might.

JUPITER
Detested prodigy!
Even thus beneath the deep Titanian prisons
I trample thee! thou lingerest?

Mercy! mercy!
No pity, no release, no respite! Oh,
That thou wouldst make mine enemy my judge, 65
Even where he hangs, seared by my long revenge,
On Caucasus! he would not doom me thus.
Gentle, and just, and dreadless, is he not
The monarch of the world? What then art thou?
No refuge! no appeal!

Sink with me then, 70
We two will sink on the wide waves of ruin,
Even as a vulture and a snake outspent
Drop, twisted in inextricable fight,
Into a shoreless sea. Let hell unlock
Its mounded oceans of tempestuous fire, 75
And whelm on them into the bottomless void
This desolated world, and thee, and me,
The conqueror and the conquered, and the wreck
Of that for which they combated.

Ai, Ai!
The elements obey me not. I sink 80
Dizzily down, ever, for ever, down.
And, like a cloud, mine enemy above
Darkens my fall with victory! Ai, Ai!

SCENE II
The Mouth of a great River in the Island Atlantis. OCEAN *is discovered reclining near the Shore;* APOLLO *stands beside him.*

OCEAN
He fell, thou sayest, beneath his conqueror's frown?

APOLLO
Ay, when the strife was ended which made dim
The orb I rule, and shook the solid stars,
The terrors of his eye illumined heaven
With sanguine light, through the thick ragged skirts   5
Of the victorious darkness, as he fell:
Like the last glare of day's red agony,
Which, from a rent among the fiery clouds,
Burns far along the tempest-wrinkled deep.

OCEAN
He sunk to the abyss? To the dark void?   10

APOLLO
An eagle so caught in some bursting cloud
On Caucasus, his thunder-baffled wings
Entangled in the whirlwind, and his eyes
Which gazed on the undazzling sun, now blinded
By the white lightning, while the ponderous hail   15
Beats on his struggling form, which sinks at length
Prone, and the aëreal ice clings over it.

OCEAN
Henceforth the fields of heaven-reflecting sea
Which are my realm, will heave, unstained with blood,
Beneath the uplifting winds, like plains of corn   20
Swayed by the summer air; my streams will flow
Round many-peopled continents, and round

Fortunate isles; and from their glassy thrones
Blue Proteus and his humid nymphs shall mark
The shadow of fair ships, as mortals see 25
The floating bark of the light-laden moon
With that white star, its sightless pilot's crest,
Borne down the rapid sunset's ebbing sea;
Tracking their path no more by blood and groans,
And desolation, and the mingled voice 30
Of slavery and command; but by the light
Of wave-reflected flowers, and floating odours,
And music soft, and mild, free, gentle voices,
And sweetest music, such as spirits love.

APOLLO

And I shall gaze not on the deeds which make 35
My mind obscure with sorrow, as eclipse
Darkens the sphere I guide; but list, I hear
The small, clear, silver lute of the young Spirit
That sits i' the morning star.

OCEAN

                Thou must away;
Thy steeds will pause at even, till when farewell: 40
The loud deep calls me home even now to feed it
With azure calm out of the emerald urns
Which stand for ever full beside my throne.
Behold the Nereids under the green sea,
Their wavering limbs borne on the wind-like stream, 45
Their white arms lifted o'er their streaming hair
With garlands pied and starry sea-flower crowns,
Hastening to grace their mighty sister's joy.

A sound of waves is heard.
It is the unpastured sea hungering for calm.
Peace, monster; I come now. Farewell.

APOLLO
        Farewell.   50

SCENE III
Caucasus. PROMETHEUS, HERCULES, IONE,
the EARTH, SPIRITS, ASIA, *and* PANTHEA,
borne in the Car with the SPIRIT OF THE HOUR.
HERCULES **unbinds** PROMETHEUS, *who descends.*

HERCULES
Most glorious among Spirits, thus doth strength
To wisdom, courage, and long-suffering love,
And thee, who art the form they animate,
Minister like a slave.

PROMETHEUS
    Thy gentle words
Are sweeter even than freedom long desired   5
And long delayed.
    Asia, thou light of life,
Shadow of beauty unbeheld: and ye,
Fair sister nymphs, who made long years of pain
Sweet to remember, through your love and care:
Henceforth we will not part. There is a cave,   10
All overgrown with trailing odorous plants,
Which curtain out the day with leaves and flowers,
And paved with veined emerald, and a fountain

Leaps in the midst with an awakening sound.
From its curved roof the mountain's frozen tears   15
Like snow, or silver, or long diamond spires,
Hang downward, raining forth a doubtful light:
And there is heard the ever-moving air,
Whispering without from tree to tree, and birds,
And bees; and all around are mossy seats,   20
And the rough walls are clothed with long soft grass;
A simple dwelling, which shall be our own;
Where we will sit and talk of time and change,
As the world ebbs and flows, ourselves unchanged.
What can hide man from mutability?   25
And if ye sigh, then I will smile; and thou,
Ione, shalt chant fragments of sea-music,
Until I weep, when ye shall smile away
The tears she brought, which yet were sweet to shed.
We will entangle buds and flowers and beams   30
Which twinkle on the fountain's brim, and make
Strange combinations out of common things,
Like human babes in their brief innocence;
And we will search, with looks and words of love,
For hidden thoughts, each lovelier than the last,   35
Our unexhausted spirits; and like lutes
Touched by the skill of the enamoured wind,
Weave harmonies divine, yet ever new,
From difference sweet where discord cannot be;
And hither come, sped on the charmèd winds,   40
Which meet from all the points of heaven, as bees
From every flower aëreal Enna feeds,
At their known island-homes in Himera,
The echoes of the human world, which tell

Of the low voice of love, almost unheard, 45
And dove-eyed pity's murmured pain, and music,
Itself the echo of the heart, and all
That tempers or improves man's life, now free;
And lovely apparitions, – dim at first,
Then radiant, as the mind, arising bright 50
From the embrace of beauty (whence the forms
Of which these are the phantoms) casts on them
The gathered rays which are reality –
Shall visit us, the progeny immortal
Of Painting, Sculpture, and rapt Poesy, 55
And arts, though unimagined, yet to be.
The wandering voices and the shadows these
Of all that man becomes, the mediators
Of that best worship love, by him and us
Given and returned; swift shapes and sounds, which grow
More fair and soft as man grows wise and kind,
And, veil by veil, evil and error fall:
Such virtue has the cave and place around.

Turning to the SPIRIT of the HOUR.

For thee, fair Spirit, one toil remains. Ione,
Give her that curvèd shell, which Proteus old 65
Made Asia's nuptial boon, breathing within it
A voice to be accomplished, and which thou
Didst hide in grass under the hollow rock.

IONE

Thou most desired Hour, more loved and lovely
Than all thy sisters, this is the mystic shell; 70

See the pale azure fading into silver
Lining it with a soft yet glowing light:
Looks it not like lulled music sleeping there?

                    SPIRIT
It seems in truth the fairest shell of Ocean:
Its sound must be at once both sweet and strange.   75

                  PROMETHEUS
Go, borne over the cities of mankind
On whirlwind-footed coursers: once again
Outspeed the sun around the orbèd world;
And as thy chariot cleaves the kindling air,
Thou breathe into the many-folded shell,   80
Loosening its mighty music; it shall be
As thunder mingled with clear echoes: then
Return; and thou shalt dwell beside our cave.
And thou, O Mother Earth! –

                  THE EARTH
                    I hear, I feel;
Thy lips are on me, and thy touch runs down   85
Even to the adamantine central gloom
Along these marble nerves; 'tis life, 'tis joy,
And, through my withered, old, and icy frame
The warmth of an immortal youth shoots down
Circling. Henceforth the many children fair   90
Folded in my sustaining arms; all plants,
And creeping forms, and insects rainbow-winged,
And birds, and beasts, and fish, and human shapes,
Which drew disease and pain from my wan bosom,

Draining the poison of despair, shall take 95
And interchange sweet nutriment; to me
Shall they become like sister-antelopes
By one fair dam, snow-white and swift as wind,
Nursed among lilies near a brimming stream.
The dew-mists of my sunless sleep shall float 100
Under the stars like balm: night-folded flowers
Shall suck unwithering hues in their repose:
And men and beasts in happy dreams shall gather
Strength for the coming day, and all its joy:
And death shall be the last embrace of her 105
Who takes the life she gave, even as a mother,
Folding her child, says, 'Leave me not again.'

ASIA
Oh, mother! wherefore speak the name of death?
Cease they to love, and move, and breathe, and speak,
Who die?

THE EARTH
    It would avail not to reply: 110
Thou art immortal, and this tongue is known
But to the uncommunicating dead.
Death is the veil which those who live call life:
They sleep, and it is lifted: and meanwhile
In mild variety the seasons mild 115
With rainbow-skirted showers, and odorous winds,
And long blue meteors cleansing the dull night,
And the life-kindling shafts of the keen sun's
All-piercing bow, and the dew-mingled rain
Of the calm moonbeams, a soft influence mild, 120

Shall clothe the forests and the fields, ay, even
The crag-built deserts of the barren deep,
With ever-living leaves, and fruits, and flowers.
And thou ! There is a cavern where my spirit
Was panted forth in anguish whilst thy pain 125
Made my heart mad, and those who did inhale it
Became mad too, and built a temple there,
And spoke, and were oracular, and lured
The erring nations round to mutual war,
And faithless faith, such as Jove kept with thee; 130
Which breath now rises, as amongst tall weeds
A violet's exhalation, and it fills
With a serener light and crimson air
Intense, yet soft, the rocks and woods around;
It feeds the quick growth of the serpent vine, 135
And the dark linked ivy tangling wild,
And budding, blown, or odour-faded blooms
Which star the winds with points of coloured light,
As they rain through them, and bright golden globes
Of fruit, suspended in their own green heaven, 140
And through their veinèd leaves and amber stems
The flowers whose purple and translucid bowls
Stand ever mantling with aëreal dew,
The drink of spirits: and it circles round,
Like the soft waving wings of noonday dreams, 145
Inspiring calm and happy thoughts, like mine,
Now thou art thus restored. This cave is thine.
Arise ! Appear !

A SPIRIT rises in the likeness of a winged child.

    This is my torch-bearer;
Who let his lamp out in old time with gazing
On eyes from which he kindled it anew
With love, which is as fire, sweet daughter mine,
For such is that within thine own. Run, wayward,
And guide this company beyond the peak
Of Bacchic Nysa, Mænad-haunted mountain,
And beyond Indus and its tribute rivers,
Trampling the torrent streams and glassy lakes
With feet unwet, unwearied, undelaying,
And up the green ravine, across the vale,
Beside the windless and crystalline pool,
Where ever lies, on unerasing waves,
The image of a temple, built above,
Distinct with column, arch, and architrave,
And palm-like capital, and over-wrought,
And populous with most living imagery,
Praxitelean shapes, whose marble smiles
Fill the hushed air with everlasting love.
It is deserted now, but once it bore
Thy name, Prometheus; there the emulous youths
Bore to thy honour through the divine gloom
The lamp which was thine emblem; even as those
Who bear the untransmitted torch of hope
Into the grave, across the night of life,
As thou hast borne it most triumphantly
To this far goal of Time. Depart, farewell.
Beside that temple is the destined cave.

SCENE IV

A Forest. In the Background a Cave.
PROMETHEUS, ASIA, PANTHEA, IONE, and the
SPIRIT OF THE EARTH.

IONE

Sister, it is not earthly: how it glides
Under the leaves ! how on its head there burns
A light, like a green star, whose emerald beams
Are twined with its fair hair ! how, as it moves,
The splendour drops in flakes upon the grass ! 5
Knowest thou it?

PANTHEA

          It is the delicate spirit
That guides the earth through heaven. From afar
The populous constellations call that light
The loveliest of the planets; and sometimes
It floats along the spray of the salt sea, 10
Or makes its chariot of a foggy cloud,
Or walks through fields or cities while men sleep,
Or o'er the mountain tops, or down the rivers,
Or through the green waste wilderness, as now,
Wondering at all it sees. Before Jove reigned 15
It loved our sister Asia, and it came
Each leisure hour to drink the liquid light
Out of her eyes, for which it said it thirsted
As one bit by a dipsas, and with her
It made its childish confidence, and told her 20
All it had known or seen, for it saw much,

Yet idly reasoned what it saw; and called her –
For whence it sprung it knew not, nor do I –
Mother, dear mother.

> THE SPIRIT OF THE EARTH
> (*running to* ASIA)
>   Mother, dearest mother;

May I then talk with thee as I was wont? 25
May I then hide my eyes in thy soft arms,
After thy looks have made them tired of joy?
May I then play beside thee the long noons,
When work is none in the bright silent air?

> ASIA

I love thee, gentlest being, and henceforth 30
Can cherish thee unenvied: speak, I pray:
Thy simple talk once solaced, now delights.

> SPIRIT OF THE EARTH

Mother, I am grown wiser, though a child
Cannot be wise like thee, within this day;
And happier too; happier and wiser both. 35
Thou knowest that toads, and snakes, and loathly worms,
And venomous and malicious beasts, and boughs
That bore ill berries in the woods, were ever
An hindrance to my walks o'er the green world:
And that, among the haunts of humankind, 40
Hard-featured men, or with proud, angry looks,
Or cold, staid gait, or false and hollow smiles,
Or the dull sneer of self-loved ignorance,
Or other such foul masks, with which ill thoughts

Hide that fair being whom we spirits call man; 45
And women too, ugliest of all things evil,
(Though fair, even in a world where thou art fair,
When good and kind, free and sincere like thee),
When false or frowning made me sick at heart
To pass them, though they slept, and I unseen. 50
Well, my path lately lay through a great city
Into the woody hills surrounding it:
A sentinel was sleeping at the gate:
When there was heard a sound, so loud, it shook
The towers amid the moonlight, yet more sweet 55
Than any voice but thine, sweetest of all;
A long, long sound, as it would never end:
And all the inhabitants leaped suddenly
Out of their rest, and gathered in the streets,
Looking in wonder up to Heaven, while yet 60
The music pealed along. I hid myself
Within a fountain in the public square,
Where I lay like the reflex of the moon
Seen in a wave under green leaves; and soon
Those ugly human shapes and visages 65
Of which I spoke as having wrought me pain,
Passed floating through the air, and fading still
Into the winds that scattered them; and those
From whom they passed seemed mild and lovely forms
After some foul disguise had fallen, and all 70
Were somewhat changed, and after brief surprise
And greetings of delighted wonder, all
Went to their sleep again: and when the dawn
Came, wouldst thou think that toads, and snakes, and efts,
Could e'er be beautiful? yet so they were, 75

And that with little change of shape or hue:
All things had put their evil nature off:
I cannot tell my joy, when o'er a lake,
Upon a drooping bough with nightshade twined,
I saw two azure halcyons clinging downward   80
And thinning one bright bunch of amber berries,
With quick long beaks, and in the deep there lay
Those lovely forms imaged as in a sky;
So, with my thoughts full of these happy changes,
We meet again, the happiest change of all.   85

ASIA

And never will we part, till thy chaste sister
Who guides the frozen and inconstant moon
Will look on thy more warm and equal light
Till her heart thaw like flakes of April snow
And love thee.

SPIRIT OF THE EARTH

What! as Asia loves Prometheus?   90

ASIA

Peace, wanton, thou art yet not old enough.
Think ye by gazing on each other's eyes
To multiply your lovely selves, and fill
With spherèd fires the interlunar air?

SPIRIT OF THE EARTH

Nay, mother, while my sister trims her lamp
'Tis hard I should go darkling.   95

ASIA
Listen; look!

The SPIRIT OF THE HOUR *enters.*

PROMETHEUS
We feel what thou hast heard and seen: yet speak.

SPIRIT OF THE HOUR
Soon as the sound had ceased whose thunder filled
The abysses of the sky and the wide earth,
There was a change: the impalpable thin air 100
And the all-circling sunlight were transformed,
As if the sense of love dissolved in them
Had folded itself round the sphered world.
My vision then grew clear, and I could see
Into the mysteries of the universe: 105
Dizzy as with delight I floated down,
Winnowing the lightsome air with languid plumes,
My coursers sought their birthplace in the sun,
Where they henceforth will live exempt from toil,
Pasturing flowers of vegetable fire; 110
And where my moonlike car will stand within
A temple, gazed upon by Phidian forms
Of thee, and Asia, and the Earth, and me,
And you fair nymphs looking the love we feel, –
In memory of the tidings it has borne, – 115
Beneath a dome fretted with graven flowers,
Poised on twelve columns of resplendent stone,
And open to the bright and liquid sky.
Yoked to it by an amphisbaenic snake

The likeness of those wingèd steeds will mock
The flight from which they find repose. Alas,
Whither has wandered now my partial tongue
When all remains untold which ye would hear?
As I have said, I floated to the earth:
It was, as it is still, the pain of bliss
To move, to breathe, to be. I wandering went
Among the haunts and dwellings of mankind,
And first was disappointed not to see
Such mighty change as I had felt within
Expressed in outward things; but soon I looked,
And behold, thrones were kingless, and men walked
One with the other even as spirits do,
None fawned, none trampled; hate, disdain, or fear,
Self-love or self-contempt, on human brows
No more inscribed, as o'er the gate of hell,
'All hope abandon ye who enter here;' [3]
None frowned, none trembled, none with eager fear
Gazed on another's eye of cold command,
Until the subject of a tyrant's will
Became, worse fate, the abject of his own,
Which spurred him, like an outspent horse, to death.
None wrought his lips in truth-entangling lines
Which smiled the lie his tongue disdained to speak;
None, with firm sneer, trod out in his own heart
The sparks of love and hope till there remained
Those bitter ashes, a soul self-consumed,
And the wretch crept a vampire among men,

---

[3] Dante: *Inferno*, Canto 3, line 9:
  Lasciate ogne speranza, voi ch'intrate.

Infecting all with his own hideous ill;
None talked that common, false, cold, hollow talk
Which makes the heart deny the *yes* it breathes,   150
Yet question that unmeant hypocrisy
With such a self-mistrust as has no name.
And women, too, frank, beautiful, and kind
As the free heaven which rains fresh light and dew
On the wide earth, past; gentle radiant forms,   155
From custom's evil taint exempt and pure;
Speaking the wisdom once they could not think,
Looking emotions once they feared to feel,
And changed to all which once they dared not be,
Yet being now, made earth like heaven; nor pride,   160
Nor jealousy, nor envy, nor ill shame,
The bitterest of those drops of treasured gall,
Spoiled the sweet taste of the nepenthe, love.

Thrones, altars, judgement-seats, and prisons; wherein,
And beside which, by wretched men were borne   165
Sceptres, tiaras, swords, and chains, and tomes
Of reasoned wrong, glozed on by ignorance,
Were like those monstrous and barbaric shapes,
The ghosts of a no-more-remembered fame,
Which, from their unworn obelisks, look forth   170
In triumph o'er the palaces and tombs
Of those who were their conquerors: mouldering round,
These imaged to the pride of kings and priests
A dark yet mighty faith, a power as wide
As is the world it wasted, and are now   175
But an astonishment; even so the tools
And emblems of its last captivity,

Amid the dwellings of the peopled earth,
Stand, not o'erthrown, but unregarded now.
And those foul shapes, abhorred by god and man, –   180
Which, under many a name and many a form
Strange, savage, ghastly, dark and execrable,
Were Jupiter, the tyrant of the world;
And which the nations, panic-stricken, served
With blood, and hearts broken by long hope, and love
Dragged to his altars soiled and garlandless,
And slain among men's unreclaiming tears,
Flattering the thing they feared, which fear was hate, –
Frown, mouldering fast, o'er their abandoned shrines:
The painted veil, by those who were, called life,   190
Which mimicked, as with colours idly spread,
All men believed and hoped, is torn aside;
The loathsome mask has fallen, the man remains
Sceptreless, free, uncircumscribed, but man
Equal, unclassed, tribeless, and nationless,   195
Exempt from awe, worship, degree, the king
Over himself; just, gentle, wise; but man
Passionless? ––– no, yet free from guilt or pain,
Which were, for his will made or suffered them,
Nor yet exempt, though ruling them like slaves,   200
From chance, and death, and mutability,
The clogs of that which else might oversoar
The loftiest star of unascended heaven,
Pinnacled dim in the intense inane.

END OF THE THIRD ACT

ACT IV

SCENE

A Part of the Forest near the Cave of PROMETHEUS.
PANTHEA *and* IONE *are sleeping:*
they awaken gradually during the first Song.

VOICE OF UNSEEN SPIRITS
    The pale stars are gone !
  For the sun, their swift shepherd,
  To their folds them compelling,
    In the depths of the dawn,
Hastes, in meteor-eclipsing array, and they flee
    Beyond his blue dwelling,
  As fawns flee the leopard.
    But where are ye?

A Train of dark Forms and Shadows passes by confusedly, singing.

    Here, oh, here:
    We bear the bier   10
Of the Father of many a cancelled year !
    Spectres we
    Of the dead Hours be,
We bear Time to his tomb in eternity.

    Strew, oh, strew   15
    Hair, not yew !
Wet the dusty pall with tears, not dew !
    Be the faded flowers

Of Death's bare bowers
Spread on the corpse of the King of Hours ! 20

Haste, oh, haste !
As shades are chased,
Trembling, by day, from heaven's blue waste.
We melt away,
Like dissolving spray, 25
From the children of a diviner day,
With the lullaby
Of winds that die
On the bosom of their own harmony !

IONE
What dark forms were they? 30

PANTHEA
The past Hours weak and gray,
With the spoil which their toil
Raked together
From the conquest but One could foil.

IONE
Have they passed?

PANTHEA
They have passed; 35
They outspeeded the blast,
While 'tis said, they are fled:

IONE
Whither, oh, whither?

PANTHEA
To the dark, to the past, to the dead.

VOICE OF UNSEEN SPIRITS
Bright clouds float in heaven, 40
Dew-stars gleam on earth,
Waves assemble on ocean,
They are gathered and driven
By the storm of delight, by the panic of glee!
They shake with emotion, 45
They dance in their mirth.
 But where are ye?

The pine boughs are singing
Old songs with new gladness,
The billows and fountains 50
Fresh music are flinging,
Like the notes of a spirit from land and from sea;
The storms mock the mountains
With the thunder of gladness.
 But where are ye? 55

IONE
What charioteers are these?

PANTHEA
 Where are their chariots?

SEMICHORUS OF HOURS
The voice of the Spirits of Air and of Earth
Has drawn back the figured curtain of sleep
Which covered our being and darkened our birth
   In the deep.

A VOICE
In the deep?

SEMICHORUS II
      Oh, below the deep.   60

SEMICHORUS I
An hundred ages we had been kept
Cradled in visions of hate and care,
And each one who waked as his brother slept,
   Found the truth –

SEMICHORUS II
   Worse than his visions were!

SEMICHORUS I
We have heard the lute of Hope in sleep;   65
  We have known the voice of Love in dreams;
We have felt the wand of Power, and leap –

SEMICHORUS II
As the billows leap in the morning beams!

CHORUS
Weave the dance on the floor of the breeze,

Pierce with song heaven's silent light,
Enchant the day that too swiftly flees,
   To check its flight ere the cave of Night.
Once the hungry Hours were hounds
   Which chased the day like a bleeding deer,
And it limped and stumbled with many wounds
   Through the nightly dells of the desert year.

But now, oh weave the mystic measure
   Of music, and dance, and shapes of light,
Let the Hours, and the spirits of might and pleasure,
   Like the clouds and sunbeams, unite –

A VOICE

Unite!

PANTHEA

See, where the Spirits of the human mind
Wrapped in sweet sounds, as in bright veils, approach.

CHORUS OF SPIRITS

We join the throng
   Of the dance and the song,
By the whirlwind of gladness borne along;
   As the flying-fish leap
   From the Indian deep,
And mix with the sea-birds, half-asleep.

CHORUS OF HOURS

Whence come ye, so wild and so fleet,
For sandals of lightning are on your feet,

And your wings are soft and swift as thought,
And your eyes are as love which is veiled not?

   CHORUS OF SPIRITS
  We come from the mind
   Of human kind
Which was late so dusk, and obscene, and blind,
   Now 'tis an ocean
   Of clear emotion,
A heaven of serene and mighty motion.

  From that deep abyss
   Of wonder and bliss,   100
Whose caverns are crystal palaces;
   From those skiey towers
   Where Thought's crowned powers
Sit watching your dance, ye happy Hours!

  From the dim recesses   105
   Of woven caresses,
Where lovers catch ye by your loose tresses;
   From the azure isles,
   Where sweet Wisdom smiles,
Delaying your ships with her siren wiles. 110

  From the temples high
   Of Man's ear and eye,
Roofed over Sculpture and Poesy;
   From the murmurings
   Of the unsealed springs   115
Where Science bedews her Dædal wings.

　　　　Years after years,
　　　　Through blood, and tears,
　　And a thick hell of hatreds, and hopes, and fears;
　　　　We waded and flew,   120
　　　　And the islets were few
　　Where the bud-blighted flowers of happiness grew.

　　　　Our feet now, every palm,
　　　　Are sandalled with calm,
　　And the dew of our wings is a rain of balm;   125
　　　　And, beyond our eyes,
　　　　The human love lies
　　Which makes all it gazes on Paradise.

　　　　CHORUS OF SPIRITS AND HOURS
　　Then weave the web of the mystic measure;
From the depths of the sky and the ends of the earth,
　　Come, swift Spirits of might and of pleasure,
Fill the dance and the music of mirth,
　　As the waves of a thousand streams rush by
　　To an ocean of splendour and harmony !

　　　　　CHORUS OF SPIRITS
　　　　Our spoil is won,   135
　　　　Our task is done,
　　We are free to dive, or soar, or run;
　　　　Beyond and around,
　　　　Or within the bound
　　Which clips the world with darkness round.   140
　　　　We'll pass the eyes

Of the starry skies
Into the hoar deep to colonize;
    Death, Chaos, and Night,
    From the sound of our flight, 145
Shall flee, like mist from a tempest's might.

    And Earth, Air, and Light,
    And the Spirit of Might,
Which drives round the stars in their fiery flight;
    And Love, Thought, and Breath, 150
    The powers that quell Death,
Wherever we soar shall assemble beneath.

    And our singing shall build
    In the void's loose field
A world for the Spirit of Wisdom to wield; 155
    We will take our plan
    From the new world of man,
And our work shall be called the Promethean.

CHORUS OF HOURS
Break the dance, and scatter the song;
    Let some depart, and some remain; 160

SEMICHORUS I
We, beyond heaven, are driven along:

SEMICHORUS II
Us the enchantments of earth retain:

SEMICHORUS I
Ceaseless, and rapid, and fierce, and free,
With the Spirits which build a new earth and sea,
And a heaven where yet heaven could never be; 165

SEMICHORUS II
Solemn, and slow, and serene, and bright,
Leading the Day and outspeeding the Night,
With the powers of a world of perfect light;

SEMICHORUS I
We whirl, singing loud, round the gathering sphere,
Till the trees, and the beasts, and the clouds appear
From its chaos made calm by love, not fear.

SEMICHORUS II
We encircle the ocean and mountains of earth,
And the happy forms of its death and birth
Change to the music of our sweet mirth.

CHORUS OF HOURS AND SPIRITS
Break the dance, and scatter the song; 175
    Let some depart, and some remain,
Wherever we fly we lead along
In leashes, like starbeams, soft yet strong,
    The clouds that are heavy with love's sweet rain.

PANTHEA
Ha! they are gone!

IONE
                Yet feel you no delight   180
From the past sweetness?

PANTHEA
                As the bare green hill
When some soft cloud vanishes into rain,
Laughs with a thousand drops of sunny water
To the unpavilioned sky!

IONE
                Even whilst we speak
New notes arise. What is that awful sound?   185

PANTHEA
'Tis the deep music of the rolling world
Kindling within the strings of the waved air
Aeolian modulations.

IONE
                Listen too,
How every pause is filled with under-notes,
Clear, silver, icy, keen awakening tones,   190
Which pierce the sense, and live within the soul,
As the sharp stars pierce winter's crystal air
And gaze upon themselves within the sea.

PANTHEA
But see where through two openings in the forest
Which hanging branches overcanopy,   195
And where two runnels of a rivulet,

Between the close moss violet-inwoven,
Have made their path of melody, like sisters
Who part with sighs that they may meet in smiles,
Turning their dear disunion to an isle 200
Of lovely grief, a wood of sweet sad thoughts;
Two visions of strange radiance float upon
The ocean-like enchantment of strong sound,
Which flows intenser, keener, deeper yet
Under the ground and through the windless air. 205

IONE
I see a chariot like that thinnest boat,
In which the Mother of the Months is borne
By ebbing light into her western cave,
When she upsprings from interlunar dreams;
O'er which is curved an orblike canopy 210
Of gentle darkness, and the hills and woods,
Distinctly seen through that dusk aery veil,
Regard like shapes in an enchanter's glass;
Its wheels are solid clouds, azure and gold,
Such as the genii of the thunderstorm 215
Pile on the floor of the illumined sea
When the sun rushes under it; they roll
And move and grow as with an inward wind;
Within it sits a wingèd infant, white
Its countenance, like the whiteness of bright snow, 220
Its plumes are as feathers of sunny frost,
Its limbs gleam white, through the wind-flowing folds
Of its white robe, woof of ethereal pearl.
Its hair is white, the brightness of white light
Scattered in strings; yet its two eyes are heavens 225

Of liquid darkness, which the Deity
Within seems pouring, as a storm is poured
From jaggèd clouds, out of their arrowy lashes,
Tempering the cold and radiant air around,
With fire that is not brightness; in its hand   230
It sways a quivering moonbeam, from whose point
A guiding power directs the chariot's prow
Over its wheelèd clouds, which as they roll
Over the grass, and flowers, and waves, wake sounds,
Sweet as a singing rain of silver dew.   235

PANTHEA
And from the other opening in the wood
Rushes, with loud and whirlwind harmony,
A sphere, which is as many thousand spheres,
Solid as crystal, yet through all its mass
Flow, as through empty space, music and light: 240
Ten thousand orbs involving and involved,
Purple and azure, white, and green, and golden,
Sphere within sphere; and every space between
Peopled with unimaginable shapes,
Such as ghosts dream dwell in the lampless deep,   245
Yet each inter-transpicuous, and they whirl
Over each other with a thousand motions,
Upon a thousand sightless axles spinning,
And with the force of self-destroying swiftness,
Intensely, slowly, solemnly, roll on,   250
Kindling with mingled sounds, and many tones,
Intelligible words and music wild.
With mighty whirl the multitudinous orb
Grinds the bright brook into an azure mist

Of elemental subtlety, like light; 255
And the wild odour of the forest flowers,
The music of the living grass and air,
The emerald light of leaf-entangled beams
Round its intense yet self-conflicting speed,
Seem kneaded into one aëreal mass 260
Which drowns the sense. Within the orb itself,
Pillowed upon its alabaster arms,
Like to a child o'erwearied with sweet toil,
On its own folded wings, and wavy hair,
The Spirit of the Earth is laid asleep, 265
And you can see its little lips are moving,
Amid the changing light of their own smiles,
Like one who talks of what he loves in dream.

IONE
'Tis only mocking the orb's harmony.

PANTHEA
And from a star upon its forehead, shoot, 270
Like swords of azure fire, or golden spears
With tyrant-quelling myrtle overtwined,
Embleming heaven and earth united now,
Vast beams like spokes of some invisible wheel
Which whirl as the orb whirls, swifter than thought, 275
Filling the abyss with sun-like lightenings,
And perpendicular now, and now transverse,
Pierce the dark soil, and as they pierce and pass,
Make bare the secrets of the earth's deep heart;
Infinite mine of adamant and gold, 280
Valueless stones, and unimagined gems,

And caverns on crystalline columns poised
With vegetable silver overspread;
Wells of unfathomed fire, and water springs
Whence the great sea, even as a child is fed,   285
Whose vapours clothe earth's monarch mountain-tops
With kingly, ermine snow. The beams flash on
And make appear the melancholy ruins
Of cancelled cycles; anchors, beaks of ships;
Planks turned to marble; quivers, helms, and spears,   290
And gorgon-headed targes, and the wheels
Of scythèd chariots, and the emblazonry
Of trophies, standards, and armorial beasts,
Round which death laughed, sepulchred emblems
Of dead destruction, ruin within ruin!   295
The wrecks beside of many a city vast,
Whose population which the earth grew over
Was mortal, but not human; see, they lie,
Their monstrous works, and uncouth skeletons,
Their statues, homes and fanes; prodigious shapes   300
Huddled in gray annihilation, split,
Jammed in the hard, black deep; and over these,
The anatomies of unknown wingèd things,
And fishes which were isles of living scale,
And serpents, bony chains, twisted around   305
The iron crags, or within heaps of dust
To which the tortuous strength of their last pangs
Had crushed the iron crags; and over these
The jaggèd alligator, and the might
Of earth-convulsing behemoth, which once   310
Were monarch beasts, and on the slimy shores,
And weed-overgrown continents of earth,

Increased and multiplied like summer worms
On an abandoned corpse, till the blue globe
Wrapped deluge round it like a cloak, and they   315
Yelled, gasped, and were abolished; or some God
Whose throne was in a comet, passed, and cried,
'Be not!' And like my words they were no more.

                THE EARTH
  The joy, the triumph, the delight, the madness!
  The boundless, overflowing, bursting gladness,   320
The vaporous exultation not to be confined!
  Ha! ha! the animation of delight
  Which wraps me, like an atmosphere of light,
And bears me as a cloud is borne by its own wind.

                THE MOON
    Brother mine, calm wanderer,   325
    Happy globe of land and air,
Some Spirit is darted like a beam from thee,
    Which penetrates my frozen frame,
    And passes with the warmth of flame,
With love, and odour, and deep melody   330
    Through me, through me!

                THE EARTH
  Ha! ha! the caverns of my hollow mountains,
  My cloven fire-crags, sound-exulting fountains
Laugh with a vast and inextinguishable laughter.
  The oceans, and the deserts, and the abysses,   335
  And the deep air's unmeasured wildernesses,
Answer from all their clouds and billows, echoing after.

They cry aloud as I do. Sceptred curse,
Who all our green and azure universe
Threatenedst to muffle round with black destruction,
    sending   340
A solid cloud to rain hot thunderstones,
And splinter and knead down my children's bones,
All I bring forth, to one void mass battering and blending,

Until each crag like tower, and storied column,
Palace, and obelisk, and temple solemn,   345
My imperial mountains crowned with cloud, and snow,
    and fire,
My sea-like forests, every blade and blossom
Which finds a grave or cradle in my bosom,
Were stamped by thy strong hate into a lifeless mire:

How art thou sunk, withdrawn, covered, drunk up   350
By thirsty nothing, as the brackish cup
Drained by a desert-troop, a little drop for all;
And from beneath, around, within, above,
Filling thy void annihilation, love
Bursts in like light on caves cloven by the thunder-ball.

THE MOON

The snow upon my lifeless mountains
Is loosened into living fountains,
My solid oceans flow, and sing and shine:
A spirit from my heart bursts forth,
It clothes with unexpected birth   360
My cold bare bosom: Oh ! it must be thine
On mine, on mine !

    Gazing on thee I feel, I know
    Green stalks burst forth, and bright flowers grow,
And living shapes upon my bosom move: 365
    Music is in the sea and air,
    Wingèd clouds soar here and there,
Dark with the rain new buds are dreaming of:
    'Tis love, all love!

THE EARTH
    It interpenetrates my granite mass, 370
    Through tangled roots and trodden clay doth pass
Into the utmost leaves and delicatest flowers;
    Upon the winds, among the clouds 'tis spread,
    It wakes a life in the forgotten dead,
They breathe a spirit up from their obscurest bowers. 375

    And like a storm bursting its cloudy prison
    With thunder, and with whirlwind, has arisen
Out of the lampless caves of unimagined being:
    With earthquake shock and swiftness making shiver
    Thought's stagnant chaos, unremoved for ever, 380
Till hate, and fear, and pain, light-vanquished shadows,
    fleeing,

    Leave Man, who was a many-sided mirror,
    Which could distort to many a shape of error,
This true fair world of things, a sea reflecting love;
    Which over all his kind, as the sun's heaven 385
    Gliding o'er ocean, smooth, serene, and even,
Darting from starry depths radiance and life, doth move:

Leave Man, even as a leprous child is left,
     Who follows a sick beast to some warm cleft
Of rocks, through which the might of healing springs is
         poured;   390
     Then when it wanders home with rosy smile,
     Unconscious, and its mother fears awhile
It is a spirit, then, weeps on her child restored.

   Man, oh, not men! a chain of linkèd thought,
     Of love and might to be divided not,   395
Compelling the elements with adamantine stress;
     As the sun rules, even with a tyrant's gaze,
     The unquiet republic of the maze
Of planets, struggling fierce towards heaven's free wilderness.

   Man, one harmonious soul of many a soul,   400
     Whose nature is its own divine control,
Where all things flow to all, as rivers to the sea;
     Familiar acts are beautiful through love;
     Labour, and pain, and grief, in life's green grove
Sport like tame beasts, none knew how gentle they could
         be!   405

   His will, with all mean passions, bad delights,
     And selfish cares, its trembling satellites,
A spirit ill to guide, but mighty to obey,
     Is as a tempest-wingèd ship, whose helm
     Love rules, through waves which dare not overwhelm,
Forcing life's wildest shores to own its sovereign sway.

   All things confess his strength. Through the cold mass

    Of marble and of colour his dreams pass;
Bright threads whence mothers weave the robes their
        children wear;
    Language is a perpetual Orphic song,   415
     Which rules with Dædal harmony a throng
Of thoughts and forms, which else senseless and shapeless
        were.

    The lightning is his slave; heaven's utmost deep
     Gives up her stars, and like a flock of sheep
They pass before his eye, are numbered, and roll on!   420
     The tempest is his steed, he strides the air;
    And the abyss shouts from her depth laid bare,
Heaven, hast thou secrets? Man unveils me; I have none.

        THE MOON
    The shadow of white death has passed
     From my path in heaven at last,   425
A clinging shroud of solid frost and sleep;
    And through my newly-woven bowers,
     Wander happy paramours,
Less mighty, but as mild as those who keep
      Thy vales more deep.   430

        THE EARTH
  As the dissolving warmth of dawn may fold
   A half unfrozen dew-globe, green, and gold,
And crystalline, till it becomes a wingèd mist,
    And wanders up the vault of the blue day,
     Outlives the noon, and on the sun's last ray   435
Hangs o'er the sea, a fleece of fire and amethyst.

THE MOON
Thou art folded, thou art lying
In the light which is undying
Of thine own joy, and heaven's smile divine;
All suns and constellations shower 440
On thee a light, a life, a power
Which doth array thy sphere; thou pourest thine
On mine, on mine!

THE EARTH
I spin beneath my pyramid of night,
Which points into the heavens dreaming delight, 445
Murmuring victorious joy in my enchanted sleep;
As a youth lulled in love-dreams faintly sighing,
Under the shadow of his beauty lying,
Which round his rest a watch of light and warmth doth keep.

THE MOON
As in the soft and sweet eclipse, 450
When soul meets soul on lovers' lips,
High hearts are calm, and brightest eyes are dull;
So when thy shadow falls on me,
Then am I mute and still, by thee
Covered; of thy love, Orb most beautiful, 455
Full, oh, too full!

Thou art speeding round the sun
Brightest world of many a one;
Green and azure sphere which shinest
With a light which is divinest 460

Among all the lamps of Heaven
To whom life and light is given;
I, thy crystal paramour
Borne beside thee by a power
Like the polar Paradise, 465
Magnet-like of lovers' eyes;
I, a most enamoured maiden
Whose weak brain is overladen
With the pleasure of her love,
Maniac-like around thee move
Gazing, an insatiate bride, 470
On thy form from every side
Like a Mænad, round the cup
Which Agave lifted up
In the weird Cadmæan forest. 475
Brother, wheresoe'er thou soarest
I must hurry, whirl and follow
Through the heavens wide and hollow,
Sheltered by the warm embrace
Of thy soul from hungry space, 480
Drinking from thy sense and sight
Beauty, majesty, and might,
As a lover or a chameleon
Grows like what it looks upon,
As a violet's gentle eye 485
 Gazes on the azure sky
Until its hue grows like what it beholds,
As a gray and watery mist
Glows like solid amethyst
Athwart the western mountain it enfolds, 490
 When the sunset sleeps

Upon its snow –

THE EARTH
And the weak day weeps
   That it should be so.
Oh, gentle Moon, the voice of thy delight   495
Falls on me like thy clear and tender light
Soothing the seaman, borne the summer night,
   Through isles for ever calm;
Oh, gentle Moon, thy crystal accents pierce
The caverns of my pride's deep universe,   500
Charming the tiger joy, whose tramplings fierce
   Made wounds which need thy balm.

PANTHEA
I rise as from a bath of sparkling water,
A bath of azure light, among dark rocks,
Out of the stream of sound.

IONE
               Ah me! sweet sister,   505
The stream of sound has ebbed away from us,
And you pretend to rise out of its wave,
Because your words fall like the clear, soft dew
Shaken from a bathing wood-nymph's limbs and hair.

PANTHEA
Peace! peace! a mighty Power, which is as darkness,   510
Is rising out of Earth, and from the sky
Is showered like night, and from within the air
Bursts, like eclipse which had been gathered up

Into the pores of sunlight: the bright visions,
Wherein the singing spirits rode and shone, 515
Gleam like pale meteors through a watery night.

IONE
There is a sense of words upon mine ear.

PANTHEA
An universal sound like words: Oh, list!

DEMOGORGON
Thou, Earth, calm empire of a happy soul,
    Sphere of divinest shapes and harmonies, 520
Beautiful orb! gathering as thou dost roll
    The love which paves thy path along the skies:

THE EARTH
I hear: I am as a drop of dew that dies.

DEMOGORGON
Thou, Moon, which gazest on the nightly Earth
    With wonder, as it gazes upon thee; 525
Whilst each to men, and beasts, and the swift birth
    Of birds, is beauty, love, calm, harmony:

THE MOON
I hear: I am a leaf shaken by thee!

DEMOGORGON
Ye Kings of suns and stars, Dæmons and Gods,

Ethereal Dominations, who possess 530
Elysian, windless, fortunate abodes
   Beyond Heaven's constellated wilderness:

A VOICE FROM ABOVE
Our great Republic hears: we are blest, and bless.

DEMOGORGON
Ye happy Dead, whom beams of brightest verse
   Are clouds to hide, not colours to portray, 535
Whether your nature is that universe
   Which once ye saw and suffered –

A VOICE: FROM BENEATH
Or as they
Whom we have left, we change and pass away.

DEMOGORGON
Ye elemental Genii, who have homes
   From man's high mind even to the central stone 540
Of sullen lead; from heaven's star-fretted domes
   To the dull weed some sea-worm battens on:

A CONFUSED VOICE
We hear: thy words waken Oblivion.

DEMOGORGON
Spirits, whose homes are flesh; ye beasts and birds,
   Ye worms and fish; ye living leaves and buds; 545
Lightning and wind; and ye untameable herds,
   Meteors and mists, which throng air's solitudes: –

A VOICE
Thy voice to us is wind among still woods.

DEMOGORGON
Man, who wert once a despot and a slave;
    A dupe and a deceiver; a decay;   550
A traveller from the cradle to the grave
    Through the dim night of this immortal day:

ALL
Speak: thy strong words may never pass away.

DEMOGORGON
This is the day, which down the void abysm
At the Earth-born's spell yawns for Heaven's despotism,
    And Conquest is dragged captive through the deep:
Love, from its awful throne of patient power
In the wise heart, from the last giddy hour
    Of dread endurance, from the slippery, steep,
And narrow verge of crag-like agony, springs   560
And folds over the world its healing wings.

Gentleness, Virtue, Wisdom, and Endurance,
These are the seals of that most firm assurance
    Which bars the pit over Destruction's strength;
And if, with infirm hand, Eternity,   565
Mother of many acts and hours, should free
    The serpent that would clasp her with his length;
These are the spells by which to reassume
An empire o'er the disentangled doom.

To suffer woes which Hope thinks infinite;   570
To forgive wrongs darker than death or night;
   To defy Power, which seems omnipotent;
To love, and bear; to hope till Hope creates
From its own wreck the thing it contemplates;
   Neither to change, nor falter, nor repent;   575
This, like thy glory, Titan, is to be
Good, great and joyous, beautiful and free;
This is alone Life, Joy, Empire, and Victory!

FINE

Symonds on Prometheus Unbound

That *Prometheus Unbound* and *The Cenci* should have been composed in one and the same year must be reckoned among the greatest wonders of literature, not only because of their sublime greatness, but also because of their essential difference. Æschylus, it is well-known, had written a sequel to his *Prometheus Bound*, in which he showed the final reconciliation between Zeus, the oppressor, and Prometheus, the champion, of humanity. What that reconciliation was, we do not know, because the play is lost, and the fragments are too brief for supporting any probable hypothesis. But Shelley repudiated the notion of compromise. He could not conceive of the Titan "unsaying his high language and quailing before his successful and perfidious adversary." He, therefore, approached the theme of liberation from a wholly different point of view. Prometheus in his drama is the humane vindicator of love, justice, and liberty, as opposed to Jove, the tyrannical oppressor, and creator of all evil by his selfish rule. Prometheus is the mind of man idealized, the spirit of our race, as Shelley thought it made to be. Jove is the incarnation of all that thwarts its free development. Thus counterposed, the two chief actors represent the fundamental antitheses of good and evil, liberty and despotism, love and hate. They give the form of personality to Shelley's Ormuzd-Ahriman dualism already expressed in the first canto of *Laon and Cythna*; but instead of being represented on the theatre of human life, the strife is now removed into the region of abstractions, vivified by mythopoetry. Prometheus resists Jove to the uttermost, endures all torments, physical and moral, that the tyrant plagues him with, secure in his own strength and calmly expectant of an hour which shall hurl Jove from heaven, and leave the spirit of good triumphant. That hour arrives; Jove disappears; the burdens of the world and men are suddenly removed; a new age of peace and freedom and illimitable energy begins; the whole universe partakes in the emancipation; the spirit of the earth no longer groans in pain, but sings alternate love-songs with his sister orb, the moon; Prometheus is re-united in indissoluble bonds to his old love, Asia. Asia, withdrawn from sight during the first act, but spoken of as waiting in her exile for the fated hour, is the true mate of the human spirit. She is the fairest daughter of Earth and Ocean. Like Aphrodite, she rises in the Ægean near the land called by her name; and in the time of tribulation she dwells in a far Indian vale. She is the Idea of Beauty incarnate, the shadow of the Light of Life which sustains the world and enkindles it with love, the reality of Alastor's vision, the breathing image of the awful loveliness apostrophized in the *Hymn to Intellectual Beauty*, the reflex of the splendour of which Adonais was a part. At the moment of her triumph she grows so beautiful that Ione her sister cannot see her, only feels her influence. The essential thought of Shelley's creed was that the universe is penetrated, vitalized, made real by a spirit, which he sometimes called the Spirit of Nature, but which is always conceived as more than Life, as that which gives its actuality to Life, and lastly as Love and Beauty. To adore this spirit, to clasp it with affection, and to blend with it, is, he thought, the true object of man. Therefore, the final union of Prometheus with Asia is the consummation of human destinies. Love was the only law Shelley recognized. Unterrified by the grim realities of pain and crime revealed in nature and society, he held fast to the belief that, if we could but pierce to the core of things, if we could but be what we might be, the world and man would both attain to their perfection in eternal love. What resolution through some transcendental harmony was expected by Shelley for the palpable discords in the structure of the universe, we hardly know. He did not give his philosophy systematic form; and his new science of love remains a luminous poetic vision – nowhere more brilliantly set forth than in the "sevenfold hallelujahs and harping symphonies" of this, the final triumph of his lyrical poetry.

In *Prometheus*, Shelley conceived a colossal work of art, and sketched out the main figures on a scale of surpassing magnificence. While painting in these figures, he seems to reduce their proportions too much to the level of earthly life. He quits his god-creating, heaven-compelling throne of mythopoeic inspiration, and descends to a love-story of Asia and Prometheus. In other words, he does not sustain the visionary and primeval dignity of these incarnated abstractions; nor, on the other hand, has he so elaborated their characters in detail as to give them the substantiality of persons. There is therefore something vague and hollow in both figures. Yet in the subordinate passages of the poem, the true mythopœic faculty – the faculty of finding concrete forms for thought, and of investing emotion with personality – shines forth with extraordinary force and clearness. We feel ourselves in the grasp of a primitive myth-maker while we read the description of Oceanus, and the raptures of the Earth and Moon.

A genuine liking for *Prometheus Unbound* may be reckoned the touch-stone of a man's capacity for understanding lyric poetry. The world in which the action is supposed to move, rings with spirit voices; and what these spirits sing, is melody more purged of mortal dross than any other poet's ear has caught, while listening to his own heart's song, or to the rhythms of the world. There are hymns in *Prometheus*, which seem to realize the miracle of making words, detached from meaning, the substance of a new ethereal music; and yet although their verbal harmony is such, they are never devoid of definite significance for those who understand. Shelley scorned the æsthetics of a school which finds "sense swooning into nonsense" admirable. And if a critic is so dull as to ask what "Life of Life ! thy lips enkindle" means, or to whom it is addressed, none can help him any more than one can help a man whose sense of hearing is too gross for the tenuity of a bat's cry. A voice in the air thus sings the hymn of Asia at the moment of her apotheosis: –

Life of Life ! thy lips enkindle
    With their love the breath between them;
And thy smiles before they dwindle
    Make the cold air fire; then screen them
In those looks where whose gazes
Faints, entangled in their mazes.

Child of Light ! thy limbs are burning
    Through the vest which seems to hide them,
As the radiant lines of morning
    Through the clouds, ere they divide them;
And this atmosphere divinest
Shrouds thee wheresoe'er thou shinest.

Fair are others; none beholds thee.
    But thy voice sounds low and tender,
Like the fairest, for it folds thee
    From the sight, that liquid splendour,
And all feel, yet see thee never,
As I feel now, lost for ever !

Lamp of Earth ! where'er thou movest
    Its dim shapes are clad with brightness,
And the souls of whom thou lovest
    Walk upon the winds with lightness,
Till they fail, as I am failing,
Dizzy, lost, yet unbewailing !

It has been said that Shelley, as a landscape painter, is decidedly Turneresque; and there is much in *Prometheus Unbound* to justify this opinion. The scale of colour is light and aerial, and the darker shadows are omitted. An excess of luminousness seems to be continually radiated from the objects at which he looks; and in this radiation of many-coloured lights, the outline itself is apt to be a little misty. Shelley, moreover, pierced through things to their spiritual essence. The actual world was less for him than that which lies within it and beyond it. "I seek," he says himself, "in what I see, the manifestation of something beyond the present and tangible object." For him, as for the poet described by one of the spirit voices in *Prometheus*, the bees in the ivy-bloom are scarcely heeded; they become in his mind, –

    Forms more real than living man,
      Nurslings of immortality.

And yet who could have brought the bees, the lake, the sun, the bloom, more perfectly before us than that picture does? What vignette is more exquisitely coloured and finished than the little study of a pair of halcyons in the third act? Blake is perhaps the only artist who could have illustrated this drama. He might have shadowed forth the choirs of spirits, the trailing voices and their thrilling songs, phantasmal Demogorgon, and the charioted Hour. Prometheus, too, with his "flowing limbs," has just Blake's fault of impersonation – the touch of unreality in that painter's Adam.

                    John Addington Symonds
                    from *Shelley*, London 1887.

PROMETHEUS
by Johann Wolfgang von Goethe
(ca. 1789)

Cover your heaven, Zeus,
With haze of clouds,
And practise on oak trees
And mountain tops, like a boy,
Who lops off thistle heads !
But you must allow
My earth to stand,
And my hut,
Which you did not build,
And my hearth,
Whose glow
You envy me.

I know nothing meaner
Under the sun, than you gods !
You pitifully nourish
Your majesty
On sacrifices
And prayer puffs
And you would starve, were
Not children and beggars
Fools full of hope.

When I was a child,
Not knowing hither from yon,
I turned my wandering eye
To the sun, as though above
There were an ear to hear my cry,
A heart like mine,
To pity the oppressed.

Who helped me against
The pride of the Titans?
Who saved me from death,
From slavery?
Did you not achieve all yourself,
Holy, glowing heart?
And you, glowing young and good,
Were you duped into thanking
The Sleeper above?

Should I honor you? For what?
Have you ever eased pain
Of the heavy laden?
Have you ever dried tears
Of those in anguish?

Was I not wrought into a man
By almighty Time
And eternal Fate,
My masters and yours?

Do you somehow imagine
That I should hate life,
Flee to the desert,
Because not all
Blossoming dreams bore fruit?

Here I sit, making men
In my image,
A race, to be like me,
To suffer, weep,
Have fun and be glad,
And to pay you no heed,
As I.

Translated from German by John Lauritsen.

The Typefaces

Text is set in Joanna, created by Eric Gill in 1930 and used by him in the 2nd edition (1936) of his classic book, *An Essay on Typography*. Inspired in part by 16th century types of Robert Granjon, yet with certain elements of modernism, Joanna is not a conventionally beautiful typeface, but it is readable, even down to the smallest sizes. Gill himself described Joanna as "a book face free from all fancy business".

Joanna was chosen for this book for several reasons. By its very plainness, Joanna does not distract the reader's imagination from the sounds and images of the beautiful Medwin-Shelley translation. With generous leading, Joanna encourages reading at an appropriately slow tempo, one at which the words can be *heard*.

In line with Gill's sentiments ("The Procrustean Bed"), the right-hand margins in this book are not justified.

Trajanus is used for the cover and title page.

The Editor

John Lauritsen is best known for his writings on Gay Liberation, AIDS Criticism, and the English Romantics. He received bouquets and brickbats for his most recent book, *The Man Who Wrote Frankenstein* (2007).

The Artist

The painting on the cover, "The Torture of Prometheus", is by the French artist, Jean-Louis-Cesar Lair (1781-1828). It was done in 1819, the same year that Shelley completed *Prometheus Unbound*.

CPSIA information can be obtained at www.ICGtesting.com
Printed in the USA
BVOW02s0448030516

446476BV00001B/2/P

9 780943 742199